SO, YOU WANT To Be a CHEF?

How to Get Started in the World of CULINARY ARTS

J. M. Bedell

ALADDIN
New York London Toronto Sydney New Delhi

BEYOND WORDS
Hillsboro, Oregon

ALADDIN
An imprint of Simon & Schuster
Children's Publishing Division
1230 Avenue of the Americas
New York, NY 10020

BEYOND WORDS
20827 N.W. Cornell Road, Suite 500
Hillsboro, Oregon 97124-9808
503-531-8700 / 503-531-8773 fax
www.beyondword.com

This Beyond Words/Aladdin edition October 2013

Text copyright © 2013 by Beyond Words/Simon & Schuster, Inc.
Illustrations copyright © 2013 by iStockphoto.com.

For information about special discounts for bulk purchases, please contact Simon &
Schuster Special Sales at 1-866-506-1949 or business@simonandschuster.com.

The Simon & Schuster Speakers Bureau can bring authors to your live event.
For more information or to book an event contact the Simon & Schuster Speakers
Bureau at 1-866-248-3049 or visit our website at www.simonspeakers.com.

Managing Editor: Lindsay S. Brown
Editors: Emmalisa Sparrow, Kristin Thiel
Proofreader: Gretchen Stelter
Design and Whisk Illustration: Sara E. Blum
The text of this book was set in Bembo.

Manufactured in the United States of America 1013 FFG

10 9 8 7 6 5 4 3 2 1

Library of Congress Cataloging-in-Publication Data

Bedell, J. M. (Jane M.)
   So, you want to be a chef? : how to get started in the world of culinary arts /
   J.M. Bedell.
      pages   cm. — (Be what you want series)
   Includes bibliographical references.
   1. Cooking—Vocational guidance—Juvenile literature. 2. Cooks—
   Juvenile literature. I. Title.
   TX652.4.B43 2013
   641.5023—dc23

                                                    2013007945

ISBN 978-1-58270-437-1 (hc)
ISBN 978-1-58270-436-4 (pbk)
ISBN 978-1-4424-8884-7 (eBook)

CONTENTS

This is my invariable advice to people:
Learn how to cook—try new recipes,
learn from your mistakes, be fearless,
and above all have fun!

Julia Child, *My Life in France*

1

Choosing a Career in the Culinary Arts

Choosing a career in the culinary arts begins with an interest in food—but it doesn't end there. You may love food and love to eat, but focusing your life's work in the culinary field is a big decision and requires some thought. There are many paths that you can take, and honestly assessing your interests and personality traits will narrow your options. Think about the five passions listed below. If one of them makes you scream, "Hey, I think that's me!" then you may want to earn a living with food.

Reasons You May Want to Work in the Culinary Arts

A Passion for Cooking Food

Do fresh fruits and vegetables make you smile? Does a list of ingredients send your mind spinning with new recipe ideas? Do you scribble down menu plans as you walk through the farmers' market? Does the smell of freshly ground spices make your tongue tingle? A passion for food combined with a passion for cooking is important if you want to pursue a career as a chef, a sous chef, a pastry chef, a baker, a caterer, or any of the other careers for which the kitchen is your workplace. Besides cooking, these careers require that you be creative and artistic. The jobs are physically demanding. Expect to work long hours standing on your feet.

A Passion for Writing about Food

Do you see a beautifully designed plate of food and immediately think of creative adjectives to describe it? Does an excellent meal end with you sharing your opinions about it with friends? When you hear about a new food product, do you immediately look for more information and want to share it with others? Do you love to experiment with recipes? If your love for food is expressed through writing, then consider a culinary arts career in publishing or other forms of media. Your future may lie in becoming a food critic, a food journalist, or a cookbook author. You may also pursue a career in television or in advertising.

A Passion for Capturing the Physical Beauty of Food

Do you look at a baked apple pie and see a thing of beauty? Does the image of a perfect cluster of grapes mesmerize you? The artist's eye is required if you're going to succeed as a food photographer or a food stylist. An understanding of color, texture, and form is also important if you want to excel as a chef, a pastry chef, or a specialty cake designer.

A Passion for Managing People and Events

Do you make lists? Does the thought of organizing a big event send you into squeals of delight? Are you a person who can multitask, manage people, and take charge in any situation without falling apart, getting angry, or collapsing under the stress? If so, then owning or managing a restaurant might be the culinary career for you. Those skills are also important if you want to own a catering business, run a food truck, or work in television. Chefs should also hone these skills if they hope to run a happy and efficient kitchen.

A Passion for Improving the Food Supply

Does the idea of preservatives in your food make you cringe? When you hear about a salmonella outbreak, does it make you want to figure out ways to prevent it from happening again? Does your heart ache for those who go to bed hungry? Not all culinary careers require that you work directly with food. If you would rather work behind the scenes or in a laboratory, consider working as a food scientist. Food scientists create new recipes, discover new ways to package foods, strive to keep the nation's food supply safe, and conduct research to improve food quality and productivity.

25 Places Where Culinary Professionals Work

1. Airlines
2. Assisted-living facilities
3. Bakeries and pastry shops
4. Breweries
5. Catering companies
6. Commissary kitchens
7. Correctional centers
8. Cruise ships
9. Development kitchens
10. Educational institutions
11. Hospitals
12. Hotels
13. Magazine and book publishing houses
14. Military bases
15. Nursing homes
16. Private households
17. Public relations and marketing firms
18. Resorts and spas
19. Restaurants

20. Retirement communities
21. Sales offices of restaurant equipment or ingredients
22. Specialty food stores
23. Television and radio stations
24. Test kitchens
25. Wineries

As you start thinking about a career in the culinary arts, it's important to consider the many ways your dream can come true. You may go to culinary school, you may be tutored by one or more mentors, or you may be trained through a variety of different jobs. In the following interview, Roland Mesnier tells how he started out as a poor, small-town boy in France and worked his way up to one of the highest culinary positions in the United States, executive pastry chef to the president.

Seasoned Profile

Name: Roland Mesnier
Job: Executive pastry chef, the White House

Awards: Antonin Carême Medal; French Knight of the Order of Agricultural Merit; *Légion d'Honneur*, the highest honor bestowed on a French citizen; member of *Chocolatier* magazine and *Pastry Art and Design* magazine's (merged and renamed *Dessert Professional* magazine) Hall of Fame

Education: Doctorate of Culinary Arts, Johnson & Wales University, South Carolina

Outside the Kitchen: Author of many books, including *Dessert University*; *Basic to Beautiful Cakes*; *All the Presidents' Pastries: Twenty-Five Years in the White House, A Memoir*; *A Sweet World of White House Desserts*

Quote by the Chef:

"You must make things happen for yourself. Don't rely on others. If you want it to happen, open the doors and do it yourself."

Quotes about the Chef:

"During our White House years together, Roland could work his magic for a small family gathering or a dinner for six hundred. Everything he ever prepared was made with love and an unfaltering dedication to the art of pastry making and the highest standards of his profession."
—Hillary Rodham Clinton

"What does Roland Mesnier make with seven pounds of chocolate, six pounds of butter, and lots of imagination? Pure perfection!"
—Laura Bush

When did you discover a love for baking and want to focus your career in that area?

I was born in the tiny village of Bonnay, France, as one of nine kids. We were very poor, with no electricity and no running water. We only had what we grew in the garden and raised for meat. Both my parents worked all day to bring home enough money for us to live. But we were loved. They were great parents, and we were a happy family. I had two older brothers in the food business. One was a baker and the other owned a pastry shop. When I wasn't in school, I had to work. I spent my summers working at the pastry shop. There

I saw all kinds of pastries being made. I was mesmerized by the transformation that happened when you took ingredients, mixed them together, put them in the oven, and pulled out a beautiful cake. I was blown away by that. I was about twelve when I knew I wanted to be a pastry chef.

Tell about your journey from working in a pastry shop in France to accepting the position of executive pastry chef in the White House.

When I was around fourteen, I left school and the pastry shop to get an apprenticeship in a bigger town. I wanted to work for someone who made really good pastries. I signed a three-year contract to work as an apprentice at the Bonnot Pastry Shop in Besançon, France. I got room and board and, for the first six months, I made about one dollar a month. For the first year, I cleaned, washed equipment, and worked in the garden. I didn't cook anything, just did lots of hard work. The owner was testing me to see if I was strong enough, tough enough to be a pastry cook. I worked long days, 6:00 AM to 9:00 PM. The young apprentices worked the same long hours as the grown men. There was no time for amusement, just work and sleep. Eventually I was allowed to make chocolates and cookies, simple jobs. Ah, but then came the day when the owner said I could bake my first cake. Finally he trusted me enough to give me his recipe and let me try. I was so proud! I had been watching others do it, and now it was my turn. His trust in me meant so much, huge.

After three years, I took the state exam, got my graduation papers, and became a pastry cook. Not a chef. Kids today think they can be a chef in six months. No, it takes ten to fifteen years to become a chef, and your salary is only enough to live on. My first job as a pastry cook was in the same city. I worked for a bigger place, a volume shop. For example, on Sundays we got to work at 1:00 AM. We made croissants, thirty-five hundred of them, for the local hotels and other businesses. From there I decided to go to Paris. I found a job in the center of the city, working in a restaurant with a pastry shop. I learned some new things, but I soon grew bored and started to research where to go next. The executive chef suggested I go to Germany and learn to work with marzipan. In Germany they know how to make beautiful decorations.

I was seventeen and didn't speak a word of German. But I left my job, my home—I had nothing—and boarded a train for Germany. I knocked on the door of a big, beautiful shop in Hannover and tried to convince them to hire me. It was hard to communicate, but soon I found a translator and that helped. I worked at that shop for one year. I learned to make chocolate candies, German pastries, ice cream, and I got a lot of new recipes. After that, I went to Hamburg, to a family business. There I learned to make different kinds of German pastries. But more important, I learned to be precise. I learned to work fast, to be spotlessly clean, and to do what I was told. No one was allowed to be cocky or they were kicked out. In the first six months of being in Germany, I learned the language and how to read and write it. I knew then that speaking several languages would be important in my career.

At eighteen I returned to France to fulfill my mandatory military service. I was in charge of guns and ammunition and new-recruit uniforms. All the while I was in the service, I was investigating where to go next. I wanted to work in a spectacular place. I chose the Savoy Hotel in London. At the time, it was number one in the world. I wrote letters to the chefs asking for a job. They said, "NO!" I wrote again. They said, "No, no." I tried again, and finally they said yes. It was a huge coup for me, and I got it on my own, no recommendations from anyone. You must make things happen for yourself. Don't rely on others. If you want it to happen, open the doors and do it yourself. By the time my service was over, I had all the paperwork done, including my work visa. I left the military on December 22 and arrived at the

Savoy on December 28. I was the assistant pastry chef at the Savoy. While there, I learned English, but most important, I learned what perfection meant. Everything at the Savoy had to be absolutely perfect. I was there for two years.

Finally it was time for me to become a pastry chef. I went to Bermuda to work at the Princess Hotel, a first-class hotel. At the time, it was privately owned by the richest man in the world. I stayed in Bermuda for ten years. I met my wife, Martha, there. Our son, George, was born and went to school there. However, over time, the island became too small for me. I wanted space; I wanted seasons. It broke my heart to leave, but it was time. Bermuda will always be home to me.

From Bermuda I went back to France and worked for a short time as the executive pastry chef at the Four Seasons Hotel George V in Paris. But I missed Bermuda and went back as the corporate pastry chef for Princess Hotel International, where I oversaw nine separate hotels. In 1976, when I was thirty-one, I came to the United States. I took a position as executive pastry chef at the Homestead, a beautiful resort hotel in Hot Springs, Virginia. During my fourth year there, White House staff started coming to the resort. Soon they were telling me that First Lady Rosalynn Carter was looking for a pastry chef; would I like the job? I said, "NO!" I was not interested in living in Washington, DC. They tried again, and I said, "No, no." Two or three times, I turned them down. In 1979 they suggested that I come to the White House for a visit, a tour, just to see the place. I agreed. What I didn't know was that they had planned for me to meet the First Lady! I was nervous, uneasy, unprepared, and, yes, a bit upset that I wasn't told in advance. We were introduced and she was the most delightful person I had ever met. Absolutely delightful! We had a short chat, and she offered me the job. I thought, *She really wants me to come.* So, I accepted, and one month later, my twenty-six-year career at the White House began.

What does the executive pastry chef to five presidents of the United States do each day?
There was no typical day. No routine, like in most places. Every day was up for grabs, anything could happen. The job isn't for everybody. There really is no glamour to it. You are there to serve at the pleasure of the president and First Lady. It's tough, stressful, and very high pressure. Your personal life and family don't matter. The job is all-consuming. Many chefs want the job; most don't last long. They either quit or get fired. I am proud to be the one who served the longest, twenty-six years. And there was great change with every administration. They were all different, and I had to adapt. It was very challenging.

How did your job change over the years?
The volume of food needed for entertaining increased. And the number of guests increased. Unfortunately, the work space stayed the same. It became difficult, requiring precise organization and planning to get everything done on time. There was less special work, more repetition.

Is it true that you never made the same dessert twice during your twenty-six years at the White House?
Yes, that's true. I had to be very creative. And I loved it! I got to choose what to make, and I made everything different. The First Family was excited to see what they would get each night. I made interesting desserts every day. It was not a good day if I wasn't challenged. I guess that's why the job was perfect for me. I thrived on the challenge. I heard that the president stopped eating desserts after I left; there was nothing exciting going on.

What were your favorite events while serving in the White House?
I loved the family celebrations, birthdays, anniversaries. They were more intimate. I mingled with the family and

felt like I was a member of the family. It was an honor to create something special and meaningful for them.

When and why did you retire from service at the White House?

After twenty-five years, I was tired. My legs were tired; I couldn't stand for all those long hours anymore. I needed to lose weight and regain my health. It was time. I left in 2004. That lasted nine months, and then Laura Bush called me back. I worked for another six months and left in 2006. She called me back again; I worked for one week and finally left for good in December 2006. That time I insisted I was done. Twenty-six years was enough.

You are an amazing culinary artist. Since leaving the White House in 2004, where have you focused your attention?

I took care of my health and lost thirty-five pounds. I've written five books. My speaking engagements have gone through the roof! I don't have an agent or a manager, but I'm really busy these days. It's all good. I travel all over, even to China, where I am an adviser to their largest food company. I do a lot of fund-raisers where I reproduce State dinners, even using replica White House china. I did teach some classes, but I do that less and less. After fifty-three years in the kitchen, it's gotten too hard to stand that long, too physical for me.

Who has helped you most on your culinary journey and how?

All my mentors. Everywhere I went to work, I had great mentors, wonderful chefs who knew their business and took me under their wing, showed me the tricks, and shared their recipes. They prepared me to enter the pastry business. They helped me to become the human being I am today. They showed compassion and a love for passing on what they had learned. Kids today need mentors more than ever. They are lost. They need someone to take them under their wing and teach them. No chef is ever self-made. Chefs are the product of those they learned from along life's journey.

What advice would you give a young person who might be interested in becoming a pastry chef?
Being a pastry chef is a great, fantastic, noble profession. You create something from live ingredients and feed it to someone. And it's filled with love. This is a difficult profession. The reality cooking shows have turned it into a circus! They aren't mentoring young people; they are deserting them, giving them a false representation of what life as a chef is really like. Young people go into the profession unprepared for the hard work and long hours. Many leave the profession and still have a huge debt to pay off. When I ended my apprenticeship, I had a clean start, no debt. Schools make money on the backs of the students. They aren't doing a good job. If you must go to school, then choose a really good one. Search your soul; make sure this is what you want to do. This profession means long hours, few rewards, and takes a lot of patience. You need experience. . . . The road to success is paved with experience.

Chef Roland Mesnier's Recipe
Quick Chocolate Mousse with Crystallized Ginger

YIELDS 6 SERVINGS

I am amazed at the number of unnecessary chocolate mousse recipes out there. Some people will make a sabayon or add butter to make mousse. As far as I'm concerned, simpler is better. There is nothing more satisfying than the combination of cream and chocolate, with a bit of crystallized ginger added for excitement. This mousse is very good on its own, served from a large bowl or spooned into individual goblets.

Although there are only three ingredients in this recipe, you must handle them carefully for the best results. The chocolate should be a little warm to the touch; otherwise, it may set before you have a chance to fold it into the whipped cream, resulting in a grainy mousse. For the same reason, let the cream come to room temperature before you whip it. If it is too cold, it might cause the chocolate to harden too quickly.

4 ounces semisweet or bittersweet chocolate, finely chopped
1 cup heavy cream, at room temperature
2 teaspoons crystallized ginger, finely chopped
6 chocolate cups (optional)

1. Pour two inches of water into a medium saucepan and bring to a bare simmer.
2. Place the chocolate in a stainless-steel bowl that is big enough to rest on top of the saucepan, and place it over the simmering water, making sure that the bowl doesn't touch the water.
3. Heat, whisking occasionally, until the chocolate is completely melted.
4. Remove from the heat and let cool until the chocolate is just warm to the touch, between 95 and 100 degrees on a candy thermometer.
5. Whip the heavy cream with an electric mixer until it holds soft peaks.
6. Add the whipped cream and the ginger to the chocolate all at once and quickly whisk together.
7. Scrape the mousse into a large serving bowl or individual goblets or pipe it into chocolate cups if desired.
8. Serve immediately or refrigerate, uncovered, for up to one day before serving.

2

Starting a Career in the Culinary Arts

So, now that you know a little about the culinary arts, you want to learn more? That's great! This field can be rewarding and challenging. As you read through this book, you'll find information about life as an executive chef, a sous chef, and a line cook, as well as many other careers within the food industry. From master chef to food critic, from owning a restaurant to working as a food scientist, the breadth of opportunities for building a career in the culinary arts is vast.

Where does it all begin? With a love for food: the look of it, the feel of it, the smell of it, the taste of it. In some culinary careers, like food photographer or food stylist, you also need a strong artistic eye. If you have the gift of gab, you might consider a career as a food critic, a restaurant manager, or a food writer. If you would rather work in the laboratory or behind the scenes, how about creating new recipes or conducting research into how food impacts human health? And of course, there's the most recognizable career path: becoming a chef.

Culinary Profession Statistics

- The restaurant industry employs 12.9 million people, almost 10 percent of the US workforce, and is one of the largest private-sector employers.

- The restaurant industry is expected to add 1.4 million jobs in the next ten years, reaching 14.3 million workers by 2022.

- Annual sales within the industry exceed $632 billion a year.

- There are more than 970,000 individual food-business locations.

- Americans spend 48 percent of their food dollars in the food industry.

- Half of all adults have worked in the restaurant industry at some point in their lives.

- 80 percent of restaurant owners said their first job in the industry was an entry-level position.

- Restaurants employ more minority managers than any other industry.

The Hierarchy of Chefs

Chef de cuisine (executive chef or head chef) means "chief of the kitchen." The chef de cuisine is in charge of everything that relates to the kitchen.

Sous chef de cuisine (deputy chef) means "sub-chief." A sous chef is second in command and works alongside the chef de cuisine. The sous chef is responsible for carrying out the chef de cuisine's orders and standing in when that person is away.

Chef de partie (station chef or line cook) means "chief of the party or group." A chef de partie is in charge of a specific station in the meal production line and specializes in the preparation of specific dishes.

Commis means "apprentice." This junior or apprentice cook is a lower-level cook who works under the chef de partie and is there to learn and help with every station's responsibilities and operations.

School or No School

Many chefs, including those interviewed in this book, began their careers by going to school. School gives you a foundation of knowledge and industry contacts who can help guide your career. However, there are notable chefs who didn't go to culinary school. Gordon Ramsay got a degree in hotel management and now is famous in both culinary circles and on mainstream media; Rachael Ray gained her experience cooking in her family's kitchen and now has her own television show, magazine, and numerous cookbooks; and Ferran Adrià started out as a dishwasher and is now considered by many to be the world's greatest chef. There's still a place within the culinary industry for those who want to climb their way to the top, but it takes hard work and determination.

5 Reasons for Going to Culinary School

1. Learn essential kitchen skills like food safety, proper knife usage, and blending spices.
2. Get a broad understanding of industry positions from line cook to head chef.
3. Gain experience with different cooking techniques, like braising and poaching.

4. Understand food theories: what happens to food when you cook it, the chemistry of food, and the effects of mixing times, cooking times, and cooking temperatures.
5. Network with others in the field.

5 Reasons for Pursuing a Culinary Career Without School

1. Feel that your time is better spent outside a classroom.
2. Think that culinary school is too expensive.
3. Have a job during school hours.
4. Work best in a hands-on learning environment.
5. Aren't looking to be a head chef or own a restaurant; you just want a job working with food.

Seasoned Profile

FOUNDED AS THE
FRENCH CULINARY INSTITUTE

Name: Candy Argondizza
Job: Vice President of Culinary and Pastry, the International Culinary Center, Long Island, New York

What are some of your everyday tasks at the culinary school?
My responsibilities vary from creating curriculum and over-seeing existing curriculum to keeping costs in line, just like

any kitchen or business. I also support the chefs, work with the students, and constantly make sure we are a relevant school with an uncompromising commitment to a quality education. It's an extremely dynamic place to work.

What do you like most about your job?

What I like most is having an impact on the lives of my staff and students in a positive way. I work with an incredibly talented group of people who collaborate and get things done.

When did you discover a love for food and want to focus your career in the culinary arts?

I grew up in an Italian-American household, and we always had great food around. I didn't realize how good that food was until I went away to college in Colorado in 1975 and was faced with dorm food. It wasn't until I got a job cooking for extra cash that I realized that this is what I wanted to do with my life. I dropped out of college after two and a half years and applied to and went to the Culinary Institute of America from 1979 to 1981.

What education/work path did you take to get where you are today?

While in culinary school, I did an externship, or short-term apprenticeship, for four months at Tavern on the Green in New York City. While still in school, I met someone who offered me a weekend job at Fiorella's Ristorante. I worked every station possible, learning as much as I could. That job led to another. My career path has been in New York City, learning from different chefs, different cuisines, and different experiences. By 1993 I felt ready to lead my own team and kitchen, so I took a job as lead chef at a restaurant called the Blue Light, which closed in 1996.

Many jobs later, I was working at restaurant called Pageant when I ran into a chef friend who was teaching at the French Culinary Institute, the former name of the

International Culinary Center. In 2000 I was hired as a chef instructor, and twelve years later, I'm a vice president.

What advice would you give a young person who is interested in becoming a chef?
My advice to any young person is to follow your dreams and never be afraid of failure.

Can you suggest some tips for success in culinary school?
I think it's important to be open to learning as much as possible. Learn from your classmates, chefs, and family. Immerse yourself in your craft. Try to read books, blogs, everything you can get your hands on. And also taste many different things, develop your palate.

What books helped you along your career path?
The books that helped me were *La Technique* by Jacques Pepin and *La Varenne Pratique* by Anne Willan.

What is your favorite cooking tool and why?
My favorite cooking tool is my Korin knife. It's sharp, sleek, and dependable.

Describe your perfect meal.
My perfect meal would be eating fish tacos that my wife and I would make and sitting on our porch on Long Island.

What do you see as future trends in your part of the culinary industry?
Food trends in the culinary world that we address here at the center are farm to table, eating locavore, exploring charcuterie and butchering, and certain aspects of modern technology. Our program is steeped in techniques, so once students know basic technique, they can do anything. Then the food trends make sense.

Chef Candy Argondizza's Recipe

Orechiette Pasta with Late-Summer Squash, Tomato Jam, and Pecorino

YIELDS 10 SERVINGS

Orechiette
454 grams "00" flour (highly refined and talcum-powder soft)
454 grams fine semolina
1 teaspoon salt
454 grams ricotta cheese
4 egg yolks
Water, as needed

Summer Squash
400 grams onions, very thinly sliced
Extra virgin olive oil
800 grams zucchini, quartered lengthwise,
    seeds removed, and cut across into 1/8-inch slices
800 grams yellow squash, quartered lengthwise, seeds
removed, and cut across into 1/8-inch slices
8 garlic cloves, finely minced
1 tablespoon fresh oregano leaves
Salt and pepper

Tomato Jam
1 tablespoon olive oil
2 shallots, very thinly sliced
20 grams ginger, peeled and finely chopped
500 grams tomatoes, skinned, seeded, and finely diced
1 tablespoon brown sugar
1 tablespoon fennel pollen (which can be bought online, in a
    gourmet grocery, or in a spice store)
1 tablespoon coriander seed, toasted and ground to
    a powder

30 grams chicken stock
Salt and pepper

To Serve
2 tablespoons of olive oil
Pecorino Romano cheese, grated

For the Orechiette
1. Sift together the flour, semolina, and salt.
2. Combine the ricotta and egg yolks.
3. Gradually incorporate the dry ingredients into the wet ingredients.
4. Add water, if necessary, to form a dough. This particular dough should be a little firm or stiff to achieve the proper orechiette small, oval shape. The word *orechiette* means "little ear."
5. Work the dough into a smooth ball and let rest, wrapped in cellophane, for 30 minutes.
6. When the dough is ready, roll a small piece of dough into a rope. Cut off 1/4-inch pieces and, using your thumb, push down and away, forming the earlike shape.
7. Cook in boiling salted water until al dente, which means firm but not hard.

For the Summer Squash
1. Gently sweat the onions in some olive oil in a sauté pan until soft and sweet.
2. Add the garlic.
3. Add the squashes, lightly season with salt and pepper, cover with a cartouche, and let steam in their own juices until soft and broken down. Taste, adjust seasoning, add oregano, and toss to combine.

For the Tomato Jam
1. Heat the olive oil in a sauté pan. Sweat the shallots and ginger, but don't let them turn brown.

2. Add the brown sugar and melt quickly.
3. Add the tomatoes, fennel pollen, coriander, and stock, and cover with a cartouche.
4. Cook slowly until all the tomatoes break down into a fairly dry puree. Do not let any color develop during cooking.
5. Taste and adjust seasoning.

To Serve
1. Put a large serving spoon of the squash mixture into a sauté pan.
2. Add the olive oil and 2 tablespoons of the tomato jam.
3. Toss to combine and heat up.
4. Add the cooked orechiette, toss.
5. Taste and plate in a warm bowl.
6. Sprinkle with grated pecorino Romano cheese.

■ ■

Education Options for Kids

You don't have to wait till you're older to do some serious learning!

Kid Cooking Camps

Kid cooking camps are popping up across the country. They are designed especially for kids who are interested in cooking and usually don't require any cooking experience. Camps range from one-day intensive cooking classes, to week-long day cooking camps, to one-, two-, or three-week residential experiences. They are often offered on weekends, during school breaks, or during the summer. The Kids Culinary Academy of Vermont is one of the premier cooking camps. Kids from around the world go there each summer to learn how to cook and to see if they want to pursue a career in the culinary arts.

High School Culinary Arts Programs

From Harry S. Truman High School in the Bronx, New York, to

Sabin–Schellenberg Professional Technical Center in Portland, Oregon, high schools across the nation are developing culinary arts programs for teenagers. The classes teach students about nutrition, basic food preparation, kitchen safety, and sanitation. Kids learn how to prepare appetizers, main dishes, and desserts. They learn skills like restaurant management by working in campus cafés or for school catering businesses. Many students get externships at local restaurants during their final semester of the program.

Education Options for Adults

It's never too early to start thinking about your long-range education.

Cooking Classes

Cooking classes don't lead to a certificate or a diploma. They are for serious and not-so-serious cooks who want to learn more about cooking and cooking techniques. Classes can range from several hours to two months.

Culinary Certificates

Culinary certificates are offered at culinary institutes, cooking schools, community colleges, and trade/vocational schools. The American Culinary Federation offers fourteen certifications. The time required can be from one month to two years. To obtain some certificates, you don't have to go to culinary school.

However, all of them require at least thirty hours of coursework in nutrition, sanitation, safety, and supervisory management. Most certificates also require a high school diploma, a culinary school diploma, and various years of experience.

Certified Culinarian: Entry-level culinary worker in a commercial facility.

Certified Sous Chef: Chef who supervises a shift or station.

Certified Chef de Cuisine: Chef of a culinary operation with final decision-making power.

Certified Executive Chef: Department head, responsible for all culinary operations in a food service business or the owner of a food service business.

Certified Pastry Culinarian: Entry-level pastry worker in a pastry food service facility.

Certified Working Pastry Chef: Pastry chef who supervises a section or shift and has considerable responsibility.

Certified Executive Pastry Chef: Department head who reports to an executive chef and must have exceptional culinary and administrative skills.

Certified Master Chef: Chef with the highest level of culinary knowledge and mastery of cooking techniques. Must already hold an Executive Chef or Executive Pastry Chef Certificate. This exam takes eight days to complete.

Certified Master Pastry Chef: Chef with the highest level of skills and mastery of pastry cooking and baking techniques. Must already hold an Executive Chef or Executive Pastry Chef Certificate. This exam takes eight days to complete.

Personal Certified Chef: Cook-for-hire chef who is responsible for all aspects of the business, from menu planning to marketing.

Personal Certified Executive Chef: Cook-for-hire with advanced skills and at least three years of personal chef experience.

Certified Culinary Administrator: Executive-level chef who is responsible for the administrative part of a food service facility, including human resources and business planning.

Certified Secondary Culinary Educator: Responsible for all aspects of the culinary arts curriculum. Must hold an advanced degree and work as an educator in an accredited secondary or vocational school.

Certified Culinary Educator: Responsible for all aspects of the culinary arts curriculum. Must hold an advanced degree with industry experience and work as an educator in an accredited post-secondary institution or military training facility.

Associate's Degree (AA, AS)

Associate's degrees are offered at culinary institutes and community colleges. An AA or AS degree is for those who want a higher level of education and more in-depth culinary training than that provided by a certificate program. Earning this degree can take up to two years of study.

Bachelor's Degree (BA, BS)

A bachelor's degree can only be earned at a college or university. Most programs take four or more years to complete. If you want to own your own business, manage a restaurant, or pursue a career in food journalism, then consider getting a four-year college degree.

Master's Degree (MA, MS)

To get a master's degree, you must first have a bachelor's degree, be accepted into a specific program, and complete two more years of study. A master's degree is for those who want to be managers, culinary instructors, nutritionists or dietitians, or researchers.

Doctorate (PhD)

The highest academic level is a doctorate. After your master's degree is complete, a doctorate can take anywhere from two to six more years of study. A doctorate is needed if you want to pursue a career in research or university-level teaching.

Sprouting **Profile**

Name: Jessica Dix
Age: 17
Hometown: Ridgefield, Washington
Job (when not studying!): Culinary arts student

When did you discover a love for food and want to focus your energy in the culinary arts?
Before I even knew I wanted to be a chef, I did a lot involving cooking. When I was in the fifth grade, they had a program where we could go into the kitchen and help serve food to the lower grade levels. I don't remember all of it, but I specifically remember serving fish sticks. When I was younger, I absolutely *hated* fish sticks, but somehow I loved every minute of being in that kitchen. It was something I constantly looked forward to. I decided to be a chef in the seventh grade, but I honestly can't remember what exactly helped me make up my mind. Looking back, it is obvious to me that being a chef was something I had always been drawn to, whether I was aware of it at the time or not.

When and how did you decide that you wanted to attend the Clark County Skills Center Restaurant Management and Culinary Arts program?

When I first heard about the program, I didn't plan on attending. I live in Ridgefield, which is far enough away that the school district only runs a bus to the Skills Center for their morning session. At my high school, band is only offered in the morning. I wasn't about to quit band, so attending the Skills Center was out of the question. Instead my plan was to apply for the Running Start program at Clark College and join their culinary program.

My mom drives the bus that transports students from Ridgefield and La Center high schools to the Skills Center. She told me about their summer-school program. Since I couldn't do the school-year program, I decided to attend the summer school, thinking that the more experience I got the better. I barely made it in. I got the last spot in the class. I loved that summer class! I wished I could do an entire school year there, but I couldn't see how it would work.

When I decided I wanted to be a chef in the seventh grade, I went crazy reading about all the possible colleges out there and found the Culinary Institute of America (CIA) in Hyde Park, New York. It was perfect and became my new big dream. And it was still my dream when I entered the Skills Center's summer program. During that summer, Chef Andrew McColley's mom was running the front of the house. When we got everything done quickly, she would take some time and tell us stories about how the Skills Center began and how Chef Andrew got to where he is now. One story she told was about a student who desperately wanted to attend the CIA but did not get accepted. Chef Andrew got the boy in, and he ended up doing very well at the school. I had not told anyone at the Skills Center about my dream of attending the CIA. But, when I heard that story, I knew the Skills Center and Chef Andrew would be my ticket to my dream. I worked with my parents and my high school to find a solution that would allow me to attend the Skills Center without having to give up the other classes I loved. The solution was that I would attend my high school in the morning, the Skills Center in the afternoon, and take classes at Clark College to complete my course requirements for graduation. Today I know the juggling was worth it. Thanks to the Skills Center, I was accepted into the Culinary Institute of America and am on my way to achieving my dream.

Describe your experiences in the program; include the things you enjoy and the things you don't like or find difficult.

Overall, my experience has been really great. It is a wonderful feeling being in a program with people that share your passion. The types of conversations I have with my classmates would make my friends at Ridgefield look at me like I was insane. At Skills, we get excited about putting together a beautiful plate or buying a new knife. We talk about knives like other people talk about cars. "I've got an eight-inch Shun Ken Onion French knife. Oh yeah! It's great. Thirty-two layers of hand-forged steel with an ebony Pakkawood handle. Super nice." For most of us, school is the only place where we get to share our passion with others who totally understand.

I'm not saying the class is perfect. I mean, we *are* talking about high school students. We don't all get along perfectly. There is drama. But like any job, we are expected to work together and are held to a professional standard. The fact that my biggest complaint is a little bit of average high school drama really speaks for itself. I love that the staff is there for us. Everything they do is geared toward trying to improve our education and help us reach our goals. One of the most wonderful things about the class is that we are a big family. It's amazing knowing you have people pushing so hard to help you get to where you want to be.

How do you juggle your culinary classes, your regular classes, and a social life at the same time?

I actually juggle more than most high school students. Besides culinary school, regular school, and a social life, I also attend Clark College, take Taekwondo classes, and play in my high school's symphonic band, jazz band, pep band, and marching band. It's tough. I'll be the first to admit that. But it's doable. There have been times that I wish I could just forget it all. I feel tired and overwhelmed. I just want to quit. But what keeps me going is remembering that I do all this because I either love it or it is a step toward my career goal. My parents have asked me why I do so much, why

don't I let something go and make my life easier. I answer the same way every time. I don't let anything go because I love it all.

Your class was chosen to make the hors d'oeuvres for Washington Governor Jay Inslee's 2013 Governor's Ball and Reception. How was your class chosen? How did you feel when you heard the news?
When I found out, I was ecstatic! It is such a huge deal to be part of that event and to have a high school program be chosen was amazing. The Skills Center worked the Governor's Ball two other times. Our chef, Andrew McColley, is very involved in the American Culinary Foundation (ACF). The Washington State ACF is in charge of the event and invited us to participate.

How did your class decide what to make for the ball and reception? What was your part in the preparation process?
The chosen theme was "Washington State," so the menu was based on that. My part of the preparation was in the grilled prawns and cranberry salsa appetizer. I was in charge of the prawns: blanching, grilling, removing the tails, and slicing them. Obviously, I wasn't the only one doing this. There were 5,000 prawns! Once at the ball, it was really cool prepping all the items and knowing that I was contributing to the feeding of 5,000 people.

Describe your experiences on inauguration day, leading up to and throughout the events.
I got to the Skills Center to help load the bus at 9:30 AM and we left for Olympia at 11 AM. We went through a few security checkpoints before getting into the area where the ball would be held. That's when setup and prep began. I was shocked by how small the prep area was, but we managed. During the event, some of us wandered around with

trays and helped pass out the appetizers. There were so many people and the room looked gorgeous. There was one ice sculpture shaped like a dragon that looked beautiful. Almost everyone slept on the bus ride home. I was asleep before we even started rolling. All in all, it was a very cool experience and I wonder what I will do in the future to top it.

Can you offer any advice to kids who are thinking about pursuing a career in the culinary arts?
Experience it. I decided I wanted to be a chef, and after working behind a line, I loved it even more. Some people don't, though. You have to be able to handle the stress, the heat, the long hours. You will be on your feet all day. I'm still in school and I can tell you now, it will be hard on your body—cuts, burns, bruises. You have to be able to not panic when a bunch of orders come in all at once. You have to be able to move. It sounds hard. It sounds impossible. But it's not. It's amazing—that moment, when you create a plate of food that is so beautiful that people want to take pictures of it.

It sounds cheesy, but I feel powerful standing behind the line, half the burners on the range full of sauté pans and the other half with pots of pasta or sauce. I feel confident when I know what I'm doing. I love the feeling of standing in an assembly line prepping one hundred fifty plates in ten minutes. Chef Andrew tells us to "plan your work and work your plan." If you do that, for the most part you can avoid panicking. I admit I panic sometimes; actually, I panic a little bit fairly often. I panic when I doubt my knowledge or my ability to do something.

One of the beautiful things about this industry is that you will never know everything because it is always growing. But that doesn't mean you can't master techniques. Learn what you're doing and why you're doing it. The smartest piece of kitchen wisdom I ever heard was,

"Cooks know how, chefs know why." If you want to work in this industry, don't strive to be a cook. Strive to be a chef.

Where do you see yourself in ten years?
I don't know the specific job, but maybe I'll be an executive chef. What I do know is that I will be in a position where I can create beautiful pieces of art through my food. I want to create something different, something people will look at and wonder how I thought of it or how I managed to create it. I will have an associate's degree from the Culinary Institute of America and I will be one of those people who go to work every day and love what they are doing.

Who has helped you most on your journey and how did he/she help you?
Chef Andrew McColley (simply "Chef" to his students) has given me the enthusiasm to learn and experience as much as I can in this field. He is my instructor at the Clark County Skills Center and everything I know about cooking can be attributed to him. He can occasionally be hard on us students, but I wouldn't have it any other way. I know that his goal is to make us the best industry professionals possible. If he knows it, he teaches it to us. Never have I had someone in my life work as hard for me as he has done to help me achieve the best future possible.

What is your favorite cooking tool and why?
My favorite cooking tool is my Shun knife. My whole life, all of the "sharp" knives in our house have been serrated. I didn't really mind until I started cooking. Then it drove me nuts. I wanted that knife for two years, but it was expensive. The only reason I have it now is because my parents and grandma pitched in and got it for me for Christmas. It is so nice. It cuts potatoes like they are butter.

Jessica Dix's Favorite Recipe
Spritz Cookies

MAKES 50 COOKIES

3 1/2 cups all purpose flour
1 teaspoon baking powder
1 1/2 cups butter
1 cup white sugar
1 egg
1 teaspoon vanilla
1/2 teaspoon almond or lemon extract
Candied pineapple

1. Preheat oven to 400 degrees.
2. In a bowl, stir together flour and baking powder. Set aside.
3. In a large bowl, beat butter for 30 seconds.
4. Add sugar and beat until fluffy.
5. Add egg and your choice of extracts. Beat well.
6. Gradually add dry ingredients, beating until well blended.
7. Do not chill!
8. Force dough through cookie press.
9. Cut candied pineapples into small chunks and place on top, in the center of the cookie.
10. Add any sprinkles or decorations you want.
11. Bake for 7–8 minutes at 400 degrees.

CHALLENGE
Quirky Culinary Quiz

1. **Which of the following foods is used in the creation of dynamite?**

   A. Chili powder
   B. Wheat
   C. Vinegar
   D. Peanuts
   E. Ginger

2. **Which of the following is a nut?**

   A. Almond
   B. Peanut
   C. Hazelnut
   D. Cashew
   E. Pistachio

3. **Pet-de-nonne is a sweet, airy fritter. The French name literally means what?**

   A. Emperor's pillow
   B. Lady's breath
   C. Dandelion seeds
   D. Cotton bolls
   E. Nun's farts

4. **German chocolate cake was named after its country of origin, Germany.**

   A. True
   B. False

5. Which of the following fruits is botanically defined as a berry?

    A. Olive
    B. Tomato
    C. Cucumber
    D. Coffee
    E. Strawberry

6. What animal's milk is used to make authentic mozzarella cheese?

    A. Goat
    B. Cow
    C. Buffalo
    D. Horse
    E. Reindeer

7. Which of the following is a kosher food?

    A. Locust
    B. Pork
    C. Shrimp
    D. Cheeseburger
    E. Snake

8. Which fruit glows blue under ultraviolet light?

    A. Apple
    B. Orange
    C. Pear
    D. Banana
    E. Plum

9. **What common condiment contains fish bones?**

   A. Balsamic vinegar
   B. Horseradish
   C. Ketchup
   D. Worcestershire sauce
   E. Mustard

10. **Kopi Luwak is the most expensive coffee in the world because . . . ?**

   A. The beans come from an extremely rare tree.
   B. The beans are roasted in a solid-gold roaster.
   C. The trees grow on one remote island in Indonesia.
   D. The beans are processed without any form of automation.
   E. The beans are harvested from the poop of a civet.

Answers

1. D, Peanuts. Peanut oil can be used to make glycerol, a primary ingredient in nitroglycerine. Nitroglycerin is the main component of dynamite.

2. C, Hazelnut. Almonds are the seeds of a drupe fruit; peanuts are a bean or legume; cashews are seeds; pistachios are the seeds of a drupe fruit.

3. E, Nun's farts. The more polite translation is "nun's sighs."

4. B, False. The name refers to a type of sweet, dark chocolate that Sam German created for the Baker's Chocolate Company in 1852. The cake is of American origin.

5. B, Tomato. Olives, cucumbers, and coffee are examples of "false berries." Epigynous berries, or false berries, grow from parts of a flower in addition to the ovary. Strawberries are not a

berry. They are an accessory fruit, which means that the fleshy part is not generated by the ovary of the flower.

6. C, Buffalo. In the twelfth century, Italian monks of the San Lorenzo in Capua monastery fed *mozza*, a cheese made from buffalo milk, along with a slice of bread, to passing pilgrims. The word *mozzarella* first appeared in 1570 in a text by the papal court chef, Barolomeo Scappi.

7. A, Locust. Leviticus 11:20–23 says, "The only flying insects with four walking legs you may eat are those with knees extending above their feet . . . the red locust family, the yellow locust family, the spotted gray locust family, and the white locust family." Some Jewish traditions do not allow the eating of locust.

8. D, Banana. Bernhard Kräutler, a researcher at the University of Innsbruck in Austria, and his colleagues discovered that bananas glow bright blue under ultraviolet light. The intensity of the blue peaks when the fruit is perfect to eat.

9. D, Worcestershire sauce. The base for Worcestershire sauce is made from anchovies, a tiny saltwater fish. The anchovies are submerged for eighteen months in a wooden tank filled with vinegar until their flesh and bones liquefy.

10. E, The beans are harvested from the poop of a civet. The civet is part of the feline family but resembles a mongoose. It eats the coffee berries, which pass through its digestive tract. The beans are not digested and eventually drop on the jungle floor. Local farmers happily collect the beans.

3

The Chef de Cuisine, Boss of the Kitchen

When you think about becoming a chef, does a celebrity chef come to mind? Rachael Ray, Wolfgang Puck, or Paula Deen? Their faces fill our television screens as they share recipes, give tips on preparing meals, and generally entertain us. They make tons of money by creating, promoting, and selling a specific brand—themselves. Joining their ranks is possible, but it will require a lot of hard work and a huge dose of luck.

Becoming a celebrity chef is not the goal of most who decide to pursue a culinary career. You love to cook. You love to discover new flavor combinations. You love to create new recipes. But most of all, you want to share your talent with others. To become an executive chef, you have to start at the bottom, learn the ropes, know the kitchen, and know the basics. Be okay with having someone constantly telling you what to do. Be a team player. Oh, and be ready to tolerate the heat: sometimes a kitchen temperature can reach as high as 130 degrees.

Once you gain the title of chef de cuisine, you've reached your goal. Everyone knows you can cook and cook well. From here, it's all about building a reputation. Your first job as chef de cuisine will not be your last. It's a starting point that opens the door to a long career working in various restaurants, developing recipes, and building a clientele. Some chefs move on to own their own restaurants, work on television, and write cookbooks, and the very best turn their name and reputation into a national brand.

Becoming the best takes a lot of hard work. Every job will be different, every position unique. As executive chef, you'll spend less time in the kitchen, leaving those responsibilities to your sous chef. But don't think your day will be short. Executive chefs often work twelve- to fourteen-hour days.

Executive chefs are responsible for everything related to the kitchen. You create menus and new recipes, manage the kitchen staff, order and buy inventory, and design how the food will appear on the plates. You train lower-level chefs to prepare their dishes properly and consistently. Executive chefs often interact with upper management and customers. You may even be responsible for the decor of the restaurant and your customers' experience from the moment they step through the door until they leave.

A Day in the Life of One Chef de Cuisine

8:00 AM   Arrive and greet the sous chef, line cooks, and other employees. Check inventory and make sure everything is fresh and ready to serve. Assign tasks to the station cooks. Decide lunch specials and teach everyone how to prepare them.

1:00–4:30 PM   Spend time in the office catching up on paperwork and emails. Create new menus and assess costs. Talk to suppliers and sample their products. Visit the markets to get fresh meats and produce. Place orders to keep inventory up-to-date.

Work on employee schedules. When necessary, meet with the restaurant owner and customers.

5:00–6:30 PM   Meet with the sous chef and line cooks. Go over the evening specials. Answer any questions about meal preparation. Meet with waitstaff, have them sample new dishes, talk about how to describe them to the customer. Find time to eat a meal.

7:00 PM   Stay near the pass-through window as the guests arrive for dinner. Call out orders and put finishing touches on each plate. Consider special customer requests and assign them to the sous chef. Note dish requests that must be declined—things to prepare for another day.

9:00 PM   Go home.

Sprouting Profile

······· EST. 1993 ·······

Name: Luke Thomas
Age: 19
Hometown: Connah's Quay, North Wales
Job: Chef Patron or Executive Chef, Luke's Dining Room, Sanctum on the Green, Berkshire, England
Awards and Honors: Springboard's FutureChef 2009; worked with many top Michelin star chefs; seen regularly on BBC Wales

When did you discover a love for food and want to focus your career in the culinary arts?

Since the age of three, I have cooked at home and had a love for good food. I used to cook with my grandmother, and then it developed into me being the cook. I took over the kitchen. By then I knew this was something I was good at and would do for the rest of my life. I took my first part-time job as a chef at age twelve. I knew I had to try and become the next big thing in the food world since I had already put so much hard work into this!

What does the owner of and head chef at Luke's Dining Room, one of the top restaurants in England, do each day?

A standard day is starting work at 7:00 AM, checking all of the deliveries and checking the quality of the produce. The team starts at 9:00 AM. That's when we do our briefing about the menu and talk about any new ideas or dishes we are going to change.

Then the cooking starts—huge pans of sauces, soups, and purées. Whilst everything is cooking away, we work on the more delicate pieces of the dish. I always work with music on too. I find if you're picking 250 pieces of parsley dress [garnish] in silence, it drives you crazy!

Then, at midday, we do a team meeting about the bookings for the evening and have staff lunch. After that I do all of the butchery and fish preparation. At 3:00 PM we have a huge clean down so everything in the kitchen is covered in hot soapy water and scrubbed, so it's immaculate to work in. The floor is hoovered [vacuumed]. Chopping boards and knives are put back in position for evening service, and then the team has a two-hour break to relax, while I filter through hundreds of emails about new suppliers and the running of the business.

At 5:30 PM we get set for service. I taste everything and get the stoves lit. Then at 7:00 PM we get the first order through. And then the madness begins. Forty-five covers [customer groups], 135 plates of food. By 11:00 PM we normally send the last dessert out and then deep clean the kitchen. Orders get processed at midnight, and the lights go off at 12:30 AM. That's when the other chefs and I go home. That's a standard day at Luke's Dining Room.

What education/work path did you take to get where you are today?

I went to Connah's Quay High School and passed eight GCSEs [General Certificates of Secondary Education, similar to graduating from high school only at a younger age, usually age sixteen], and I also studied at Yale College Wrexham in catering and hospitality, and earned City & Guilds qualifications. [City & Guilds qualifications are recognized worldwide by employers, educational institutions, and associations as proof of skills and knowledge.]

How did you juggle both work and school?

It was crazy! I would go to school early to get my homework and extra coursework complete and then do my five lessons a day. Straight after school, I would head to the kitchens of Soughton Hall or the Chester Grosvenor [hotels in England].

Who has helped you most on your journey and how?

My cookery teacher, Mary Richmond. She took me everywhere to make things possible. She mentored me through competitions and helped raise sponsorship for me to go on work placements. She even took me to the Fat Duck so I could work with Heston Blumenthal [a three-star Michelin restaurant in Bray, Berkshire, England] for a week while my school was closed for summer.

What advice would you give a young person who is interested in becoming a chef?

Be confident and don't be scared to be different. A lot of

people judged me when they found out I was opening a restaurant at age eighteen, but I said nothing but, "Please come and eat my food, and you'll see why I'm doing this." The reviews from critics like Jay Rayner prove it's working, and working very well! It's a tough industry, and the hours are long, but if you're dedicated and passionate, it will work.

What is your favorite cooking tool and why?
The most used piece of equipment is my blender. I love making soups, purées, marinades, and dressings. I use it all the time.

Describe your perfect meal.
Good, simple British food: a nice piece of Welsh rib eye, medium rare with a peppercorn sauce. That's my favorite type of food when I'm away from the kitchen.

What do you see as future trends in your part of the culinary industry?
I think simple cooking and simple food. I think it got to a stage where people were complicating every element on the plate. The key is, if you have good-quality ingredients, keep it simple and cook them well.

Chef Luke Thomas's Signature Recipe

Crispy Duck Salad

YIELDS 4 SERVINGS

2 duck legs
Salt and white pepper
1 red onion, peeled, sliced into thin rings
100 milliliters white wine vinegar

20 grams sugar

1 Chinese grapefruit (also called a pomelo and is sweeter than regular grapefruit), skin and pith removed

2 pink grapefruits, skin and pith removed

1 bottle sweet honey mustard dressing

1 pack [bunch of] watercress

200 grams mixed leaves [greens]

1. Heat oven to 300 degrees Fahrenheit/150 degrees Celsius.
2. Season the duck legs with salt and white pepper and then place them on a rack with a tray underneath to catch excess fat.
3. Bake for two to three hours until soft or until the meat easily pulls away from the bone.
4. Remove from the oven and cool.
5. Season the onions with salt and let stand for 10 minutes.
6. Wash the salt off the onions and place them in a pan with the white wine vinegar and sugar.
7. Bring to just below boiling temperature.
8. Remove from heat and place in a container to cool. Set aside.
9. Separate the grapefruit flesh into segments. Cut between the membranes and catch the juice in a bowl. Discard the membranes. Set the juice aside.
10. Remove the skin from the cooled duck legs and discard.
11. Gently flake all of the flesh into a bowl.
12. In a large frying pan, add a tablespoon of the reserved duck fat and heat until it starts to lightly smoke.
13. Add the flaked duck and fry until crispy.
14. Place the rinsed watercress, red onion, mixed leaves [greens], and grapefruit juice into a bowl and toss.
15. Pour enough of the dressing to coat the ingredients lightly and toss again.
16. Portion the dressed leaves onto four plates.
17. Top with the warm, crispy duck.

MARIE-ANTONIN CARÊME (1784–1833), KING OF CHEFS AND CHEF OF KINGS

Marie-Antonin Carême was born in Paris, France. At the height of the French Revolution, his family kicked him out of the house. Abandoned and penniless, ten-year-old Carême wandered aimlessly until he was rescued by the owner of a shabby little restaurant. He worked as a kitchen boy in exchange for room and board. In that restaurant, he learned the rudimentary skills needed to be a cook.

When she turned fourteen, Carême became the apprentice to Sylvain Bailly, a well-known pastry cook with a bakery in one of the most fashionable neighborhoods of the city. Bailly immediately recognized Carême's talent with pastries and encouraged him to learn and experiment. Carême eventually opened his own shop, the Patisserie de la Rue de la Paix.

Going pro

In 1976 the American Culinary Federation successfully lobbied the US Department of Labor to change its designation of executive chef from the service category to the professional category in its *Dictionary of Occupational Titles*.

Carême's reputation grew. He became famous throughout Paris for the elaborate centerpieces he made from sugar, marzipan, and pastry. He designed centerpieces for Charles Talleyrand, a French diplomat, and other members of Parisian society. When Napoleon Bonaparte purchased the Château de Valençay and turned it into a gathering place for diplomats, he hired Carême to work for him there.

After the fall of Napoleon, Carême went to London. He worked for the prince regent, who later became King George IV. He also worked for Tsar Alexander I of Russia and a well-known banker named James Mayer Rothschild.

Throughout his career, Carême invented sweet nougats, meringues, croquantes, and solilemmes. He is credited with being an early supporter of haute cuisine, a grand style of cooking favored by the royals and the newly rich in eighteenth-century France. He wrote three pastry cookbooks and his masterpiece on cookery, *L'art de la Cuisine Française au XIXe Siècle*. Many consider Carême one of the first international celebrity chefs. He died in Paris at the age of forty-eight.

....

Chefs' Perspectives

Chefs Allen Routt, of The Painted Lady (page 62), and Paul Bachand, of Recipe (page 49), share their thoughts on creating menus. Interviews with both come later in the book.

Creating Menus

Chef Allen Routt often wakes up thinking about menu items. He shares his ideas with his wife, Jessica Bagley-Routt, who is also a chef. That starts the process of brainstorming about what flavors will work together. They take into consideration the season and what fruits and vegetables are at their peak of flavor. As they explore broad concepts, they add and subtract ideas, and use trial and error until they come up with the skeleton of the menu. "Listen to the ingredients and hear what they are trying to tell you" is Chef Allen's advice.

Chef Paul Bachand adjusts his menu to the seasons too. When he's visiting the farms or talking to the farmers, a dish will pop into his head. Since there are seemingly hundreds and hundreds of recipes floating around in his head, he pulls out the one that most closely matches the dish he's been thinking about. From that first dish, he develops a style for that week's menu. He combines textures, flavors, and the dish's overall appearance, which is very important to him. The fresh and new feelings of spring and summer elicit ideas for salads, vegetable dishes, and lighter ways of cooking. When fall and winter arrive, Bachand turns to slow-cook methods. He makes hearty soups and dishes that bring forth a feeling of comfort and warmth. Most of the time, his printed menus are vague, so he can tweak the dish as the week progresses.

Creating New Recipes

When Routt has a new menu item that requires a new recipe, he gets to work. He gathers the main ingredients and goes into the kitchen where he plays around, pairing ingredients and blending spices. After a few attempts, he has a good idea of where he's going with the dish. He writes down every ingredient he used, how much he used, and the sequence in which he used them. When he's finished, he checks the taste and then hands the recipe and the finished dish to his sous chef. The sous chef makes the dish again, checking every detail. If the dish is acceptable to both Routt and his sous chef, they pass it along to the line cook. The line cook makes the dish a couple more times, streamlining the process as he goes along. When he's done, he presents the finished product to the head staff, and everyone signs off on it. It's finally ready for its debut to the customer.

Bachand writes his recipes in his head. He thinks that any chef who knows his stuff knows what a new recipe will taste like. He also can envision how all the flavors will work together and knows what it will look like on the plate. After the idea is formed, he goes into the kitchen and makes the dish. He plays with different ingredients to see if he can make it even better. Once he's satisfied, he presents it to the staff and goes over how it's prepared. Since he's the one who does the cooking, most recipes stay in his head. Ninety percent of his recipes are constantly evolving, but he does write down the main, basic ones in a recipe book.

Designing Plates

Routt's goal when designing a plate is to offer his customers something that challenges their senses. First, give them something familiar, but in a different way, whether that be a different flavor, a different look, or a different pairing of ingredients. Then he focuses on the shapes and how they look together, hoping to balance everything so it is aesthetically pleasing.

Bachand likes balance. With a dish in mind, he chooses a plate to put it on: round for sharp-edged dishes, like a serving of lasagna, and square or rectangle for soft-edged dishes, such as a soufflé or pasta. He takes into consideration texture, size, color, and shape. He loves vegetables that can take different shapes according to his needs, like carrots that can be cut into long, thin slices or short, round slices.

Five Mother Sauces

There are five main sauces that are used in every kitchen. Four of the sauces—béchamel, espagnole, tomato, and veloute—were made famous by the nineteenth-century chef Marie-Antonin Carême. The fifth sauce, hollandaise, was added to the list in the twentieth century by Chef Auguste Escoffier.

Béchamel: Given its name by an unknown court chef who wanted to honor Louis de Béchamel, Marquis de Nointel. Béchamel is a white sauce made of milk thickened with white roux, which is a thickening agent made from flour and butter. Often it is flavored with nutmeg, bay leaf, onion, or cloves. It is commonly served over pastas, chicken, fish, and eggs.

Espagnole: The word *espagnole* was seen in published works as early as the eighteenth century. The name is in honor of the Spanish, whom the French of the time thought of as brown-skinned. Espagnole is a brown sauce made using roasted veal stock thickened with brown roux. Often it is flavored with thyme, parsley, or tomato paste. It is commonly served over roasted lamb, beef, duck, and veal.

Tomato: Ancient South Americans were the first to create a tomato sauce, similar to today's salsa. They added peppers, diced vegetables, and chilies to create a spicy concoction. Tomato sauce is made using tomatoes that are cooked and then pureed, reduced, or thickened using roux. Often tomato sauces are flavored using garlic, salt pork, or a bit of sugar. It is commonly served over pasta, vegetables, polenta, and chicken.

Velouté: In English, the word means "velvety." Introduced in the early nineteenth century, velouté is a white sauce made from veal, chicken, or fish stock that is then mixed with roux. This sauce is used as a base for many other sauces. It is commonly served over eggs, pasta, veal, and chicken.

Hollandaise: The earliest known version of this sauce dates back to 1758, when it was mentioned in François Marin's recipe book, *Les Dons de Comus*. The sauce was named in honor of Holland, where French chefs thought the best butter and eggs came from. Hollandaise sauce is made by emulsifying egg yolks and butter. It is often flavored with pepper, vinegar, or lemon juice and is served over eggs, asparagus, and fish.

CHALLENGE
Create a Tasty Sauce

Every culinary student must learn to make the five basic sauces.

1. Choose one of the five sauces.
2. Find a basic recipe and make it.
3. Think of three different ways you could improve on that basic sauce.
4. Make those three new sauces.
5. Write down your new sauce recipes.

Congratulations! You now have four new recipes in what will one day become your huge recipe collection.

RECIPE
A NEIGHBORHOOD KITCHEN

Name: Paul Bachand
Job: Owner and chef, Recipe: A Neighborhood Kitchen, Newberg, Oregon

When did you discover a love for food and want to focus your career in the culinary arts?

At about the age of six, I started working in a restaurant called The Hobbit. The owner and chef was a friend of my parents. He taught me to cook in the classical French style. I learned the fundamentals of cooking sauces, rolling out dough, just about everything. He paid me to work but, of course, it was all under the table. I worked there until I was about fifteen and then moved on to other jobs in local restaurants.

What education/work path did you take to get where you are today?

I knew from an early age that I wanted to go to culinary school, so I went right after high school. I wanted to get away from home, and I had friends in the area, so I applied to and was accepted at the Western Culinary Institute in Portland, Oregon. I was younger than most of my class-mates. The institute was a good school at a reasonable cost. They taught using a hands-on approach, and the student-to-teacher ratio was around ten to one.

I jumped right in and started swimming. While other kids blew off the work, I didn't. Cooking is in my blood. It was an organic progression. I grew up cooking. I love cooking. I don't know anything else.

School taught me the basics. From there I worked at a lot of different places: golf courses; small, intimate restaurants; and high-volume places that served three hundred to four hundred people a night. I experienced different styles of restaurants and many different cuisines. For the last eight years, I've focused on an artisan style, slow-cooked food made from scratch. I know what's going into the food I make. Working this way gives me a sense of satisfaction. I feel better as a chef, and it challenges me—keeps me learning.

When did you first decide that you wanted to own your own restaurant?
I opened three other restaurants in the Willamette Valley for other people. I waited until the time was right. I knew that I wanted my restaurant to be a small, intimate setting, forty to forty-five seats. No "turn and burn"—I wanted to let people sit and enjoy their meal. And it had to be in a place I loved. A place where I knew I wanted to stay.

My investor and I watched this place for a while. The previous owner couldn't make it work and when that restaurant failed, we took over. We did the renovation work ourselves. We were lucky—it took a minimal amount of investment money, and we were able to pay that back in six months. It was only three months from the time we signed the lease until opening day.

Why did you decide to open a restaurant in Newberg, Oregon?
I saw a void in the quality and value of restaurants in the area. There was a need for a place with a comfortable atmosphere, a feeling of home. I know the people in this area, what they are looking for. I wanted to fill that void.

What does an average day look like for you?

9:00 AM   On my way to work, I often stop at local farms. I like to get to know the farmers, what they grow, and how they grow it. I like supporting local farmers and look for ones who use sustainable farming methods.

10:00 AM   I get to the restaurant and start preparing for lunch. I make sure my staff has everything they need for the day, including the knowledge and tools to meet our guests' needs. While I'm cooking, I come up with new menu ideas.

11:30 AM   We open for lunch. I cook, so I'm in the kitchen the entire time. After lunch, I catch a bite to eat and start preparing for dinner. This is when I sometimes get the chance to try out new recipes, play with my food.

5:00 PM   Dinner starts on the dot! Again, I cook, so I'm in the kitchen. I interact with the guests when I can, but it isn't always possible.

9:00 PM   When the last guest is gone, we clean up and go home.

What do you like most about your job?
I like the creative side, adapting meals to the changing seasons, exemplifying the seasons in the textures and flavors of the food. That's important. My staff is important to me. I want to create the feeling of family.

What do you like least about your job?
The long summer hours. I work seventy-five to eighty hours a week. It's exhausting. But I know it will eventually end, when the cool weather and the rains come.

How do you balance the demands of owning a restaurant with family life?

Sometimes I succeed, and sometimes I don't. If I'm stressing out, my staff stresses out and that makes everyone unhappy. I keep the same two days off. When I'm not working, I like to do some remodeling on my house. That gives me a sense of accomplishment. I also like to go camping and have friends over for wine and dinner.

What advice would you give a young person who is interested in becoming a chef and eventually owning a restaurant?

Start early. Don't jump into going to school. Work in a kitchen and see what it's like. Talk to chefs. Try it out and see if you like it. You have to be able to accept criticism and critique. This business will eat you alive if you can't. Ninety-five percent hate it, five percent love it. It's a satisfying career for the five percent who embrace all aspects of it, have a passion for it. But it's not for everyone. Restaurants fail because the people who open them don't know what they are getting into.

Know that even if you go to culinary school, you will start at the bottom, maybe even washing dishes. Schools

---

The Chef as Teacher

Chefs can find full-time positions as teachers in high school culinary programs, college and university culinary programs, and culinary institutions, or part-time work as cooking instructors in gourmet kitchen stores or upscale supermarkets or teaching recreational cooking courses. Taking short-term personal chef assignments or teaching private individuals how to cook also brings in additional income.

promise too much. They are expensive. If this isn't the right career for you, it's a waste of money.

What's your favorite cooking tool and why?
I like my wooden spoon—well, spoons in general. I can use it for anything, including detail work. It's an organic piece, an extension of my hand.

Describe your perfect meal.
It would be a slice of terrine, a simple roasted chicken, fresh vegetables, and comté cheese—not dessert, just the cheese. And a bottle of Vouvray. I'd be in France with my wife. Anywhere, rural or city, it's all quaint, old, and amazing. I love the wine, food, and the people.

Sprouting **Profile**

OREGON CULINARY INSTITUTE

Name: Maya Carlile
Age: 23
Hometown: Eugene, Oregon
School: Oregon Culinary Institute

When did you discover a love for food and want to focus your energy in the culinary arts?
I grew up with parents who emphasized family dinners and home-cooked meals. They served lots of different foods,

including fresh produce, and encouraged me to help cook meals. By the time I was twenty, I knew that I really loved food. I loved talking about it, making it, and working in the restaurant industry. By then, it just made sense for me to take steps, go to school, to become more proficient and confident in culinary arts.

When and how did you decide that you wanted to attend the Oregon Culinary Institute?
After graduating from high school, I took a couple years off. Eventually, I decided to take some general education and art classes at the local community college. Nothing really caught my interest or sparked any passion, and I couldn't see myself paying tuition for an education that led nowhere. I had thought of culinary school but hadn't researched schools outside of Eugene.

After deciding that I wanted to go to culinary school, I started researching the ones in the Portland area. After phone interviews and tours, it was obvious to me that the Oregon Culinary Institute cared about individual students and would provide the experiences that I was looking for.

Describe your experiences in the program; include the things you enjoy and the things you don't like or find difficult.
My experiences in the Culinary Diploma program have been great and numerous. Time has been absolutely flying by, and I can't believe how much I've done. I've experimented with many products and succeeded and failed with many recipes. I have had endless opportunities to volunteer for culinary jobs, work special events, and gain work experience through externships. Best of all is the amount I've learned from all the chefs. It isn't always easy, but it is very rewarding and has given me the confidence I need to leave school and find a job.

What do you enjoy cooking the most and why?
I like making soups and sauces, but right now I'm focusing on getting all the hands-on experience with different products that I can. Although I don't consider myself a baker, I really like to experiment with making bread. Sometimes it comes out in a perfect, fluffy, delicious homemade loaf, but other times it literally falls flat. It can be frustrating, but I find spending all day working with and kneading dough cathartic.

How do you juggle your culinary classes with other activities and a social life?
I think you get out of school what you put into it. During the months I've been at the Institute, I've had a pretty limited social life. I go to school in the morning, ride the bus home, do my homework, and then go to work. On the days I don't work, I usually get ahead with homework, cook something new, go for a hike if the weather permits, or get together with friends for a few hours. I'm putting all I can into this short six-month program. My skills are developing. I'm gaining experience. My social life can wait.

Where do you see yourself in ten years?
Cooking at a place that makes me happy while trying new foods and recipes. I'd also like to travel.

Can you offer any advice to teens who are thinking about pursuing a career in the culinary arts?
Don't let failed recipes or kitchen mishaps discourage you. They will happen, throughout school, work, and home cooking. But failure is half the fun. Nicking yourself with your knife, overcooked such and such, or burned whatever—they are all learning experiences. You definitely learn to cook through trial and error.

Who has helped you most on your journey and how?
For five years I worked at a retirement home. I started out as a waitress and moved on to work as a prep cook. The chef in the kitchen helped get me started and encouraged me to pursue a culinary career. He had a very strict budget and had to cater to the palates and dietary restrictions of the retirees. Despite the budget restrictions, he experimented with different recipes. I respect how much passion he has for food and his ability to expose the residents to new and sometimes exotic cuisines.

What is your favorite cooking tool and why?
The cast-iron skillet. It gets really hot, holds the heat, and I can cook or bake anything and everything in it.

4

The Sous Chef, Second in Command

The French word *sous* means "under." As second in command of the kitchen, you work closely with the executive chef. Your relationship, apprentice to mentor, is important to the smooth running of the kitchen, to the restaurant's success, and to the advancement of your career. Sous chefs spend most of the day in the kitchen, so a key requirement of the job is being comfortable in that high-stress, high-energy environment.

Becoming a sous chef is a hallmark achievement. When you reach this point, celebrate! It is the last step before becoming an executive chef. The responsibilities of this position vary, but there are some general duties. Since the kitchen is your castle, sous chefs train staff, assign station duties, control inventory and food costs, watch for sanitation and safety issues, maintain kitchen equipment, suggest wine to go with menu items, and help decide daily menus and special dishes. Because it's important that every dish come out of the kitchen perfectly, the sous chef must coordinate all the station cooks so that each part of a meal is completed at the same time.

Eliana Cooks!

Name: Eliana de Las Casas
Age: 12
Hometown: Harvey, Louisiana
Job (when not studying!): owner, website Eliana Cooks!;
host, *Cool Kids Cook* radio show on VoiceAmerica Kids
Network; author, *Eliana Cooks! Recipes for Creative Kids* and
Cool Kids Cook: Louisana

When did you discover a love for food and want to focus your energy in that area?

I started cooking when I was four years old. Every Christmas
and birthday, I would ask for cooking utensils or something
related to the kitchen. At eight years old, I began my blog,
posting recipes, and food photos, and then cooking tutorial
videos for kids. I released my first cookbook, *Eliana Cooks!
Recipes for Creative Kids*, in October 2010. At the same time,
I was chosen as one of thirteen Latinos in the New Orleans
area to be featured in a Southern Food and Beverage
Museum exhibit called "New Orleans con Sabor Latino,"
which means "New Orleans with Latin Flavor."

As a food blogger and cookbook author, what is a typical day like for you?

Every day, I think about food and recipes. I am always on the lookout for new ideas. I watch cooking shows and Internet videos. I also collect cookbooks and cooking magazines. I cook about three to five times a week at home, developing new recipes for my weekly radio show, *Cool Kids Cook* on VoiceAmerica Kids Channel, and my upcoming cookbooks.

How do you juggle both work and school?
School always comes first, and I make sure I do my homework and projects before going into the kitchen. I am a good student and feel that school is very important.

Can you offer some tips for writing a successful blog?
Being consistent and doing weekly posts is important. I also share my posts via social media networks such as Twitter and Facebook. In addition, I have an app where I can blog straight from my phone, even adding photos that I have taken. It makes it so much easier, especially when I am on the road.

Tell us about your cookbook and how you chose the recipes in it.
My newest cookbook, *Cool Kids Cook: Louisiana*, features recipes from the Louisiana part of my heritage. My grandparents and mom taught me how to cook, and my book is a celebration of food and family. The book started out with a ton of recipes that we had to whittle down to just over twenty-five recipes. Choosing which recipes to include in the cookbook was a challenge.

You have a weekly radio show. How did that come about, what's it like to be on the radio, and how do you choose your topics?
In the summer of 2012, I was interviewed by one of VoiceAmerica's kid radio shows. After the interview, the producer offered me my own show! Since then, it has really grown, and I have thousands of weekly listeners. I interview top chefs, food stylists, photographers, and movers and

shakers in the culinary industry. I also have segments such as Spice Detective, where I investigate a particular spice each week and give a recipe featuring that ingredient.

Where do you see yourself in ten years?

I see myself with a cooking show on television, a series of cookbooks, and lines of spices, chef clothing for kids, and cookware designed especially for kids. I want to promote my mission of educating kids about good food and learning to cook so they can live a balanced lifestyle.

Who has helped you most on your journey and how?

My mom has been instrumental in helping me build my cooking career. She is an author and knows a lot about the publishing industry. She gives me marketing and business advice because, as a working chef, you have to be business-minded as well as creative.

What is your favorite cooking tool and why?

I love my chef's knife. I can do so much with it. I want to stress that kids should not use knives unless they have had proper training and a grown-up is there to supervise them.

Describe your perfect meal.

My perfect meal would be tacos topped with my own recipe, Guacamole and Fresh-from-the-Garden Salsa, in my own homemade tortillas. Tacos are my favorite food, and you can make so many different variations. To end the meal, I'd have a creamy serving of flan. Yum!

Eliana de Las Casas's Favorite Recipe
Fresh-from-the-Garden Salsa

3 medium tomatoes, diced
2 tablespoons onion, finely chopped

1 tablespoon cilantro, finely chopped

1 clove garlic, minced

1/2 teaspoon chopped jalapeños

1/2 teaspoon cumin

1/4 teaspoon salt

1 teaspoon lime juice

1. Mix all the ingredients in a bowl for a chunky salsa. If you prefer smooth salsa, blend all the ingredients in a food processor.

A Day in the Life of One Sous Chef

6:30 AM   Spend time at the local farmers' market and confirm orders to be dropped off later in the day.

7:00 AM   Arrive at the restaurant and change into my chef's whites. Greet everyone in the kitchen and check to see that the kitchen and every station are spotless.

9:00 AM   Check emails, work on paperwork, and confirm inventory orders for the day. Create inventory orders for tomorrow. If time allows, do some prep work or experiment with new menu items. When the head chef is ready, review the day's menus.

11:00 AM   Lunch begins. Oversee all meals leaving the kitchen, making sure every customer gets what was ordered. When the lunch rush is over, clean up the mess left on the line.

1:30 PM   Prepare the staff's meal. Take a break and eat. After lunch, meet with the head chef and work on

creating future menus, discuss new recipes, and cover the issues of the day.

2:30 PM   Greet the second shift and go over the night's reservations, specials, and events. Answer questions. Work with the head chef on preparations for the evening menu. Write down everything the cook says is needed for the next day and start a prep list for tomorrow.

4:00 PM   Conduct a preshift meeting with the front-of-house staff. Go over the evening menu specials. Have them taste new items, educate them on any new flavors, and offer suggestions for wine pairings.

5:00 PM   Walk the dry storage and coolers to make sure everything is in order for the next morning. Make necessary orders by emailing or texting farmers and vendors directly.

6:00 PM   Make sure that everything is ready for dinner and say good-bye to the crew. The work day is done.

ANCIENT RECIPES

The oldest written recipes in the Western world were found on clay tablets that date back to 1700 BC. They were written by ancient scribes and are now housed in Yale University's Babylonian Collection. Three of the tablets, referred to as the Yale Culinary Tablets, were decoded by French archeologist and chef Jean Bottéro (1914–2007). Bottéro, who decoded the text in the 1980s, wrote that the cuisine of that era was "of striking richness, refinement, sophistication, and artistry. . . . We would not have dared to think a cuisine 4,000 years old was so advanced."[1]

In the tablet's text, the Mesopotamian chefs give credit to the Assyrians and the Elamites for some of the recipes. The first tablet records twenty-one recipes, some for meat broth and some for vegetables. The second tablet has seven more complete recipes, along with instructions for cooking and presenting the dishes. The third tablet holds three partial recipes.

The code was difficult to crack, but once Bottéro found the key, he wrote a new chapter in the history of food. He helped scholars understand that ancient peoples loved food and delighted in the preparation, presentation, and consumption of it as much as we do today.

JAMES BEARD AND THE JAMES BEARD FOUNDATION AWARDS

James Andrew Beard was born in 1903 and grew up in Portland, Oregon. His mother had a passion for food that she passed on to her son. She introduced him to many new flavors by cooking meals using whatever was available.

As a young man, Beard wandered, looking for his place in the world. He attended Reed College, traveled the country with a theatrical group, studied voice and theater abroad, and tried to get parts in movies. This failed to provide a living, so in 1935 he started a catering business. He opened a shop in New York City called Hors d'Oeuvre, Inc. As his business grew, so did his passion for cooking. Finally he had found his life's work.

During World War II, he enlisted in the navy and served in the United Seamen's Service. He helped set up sailors' canteens in several countries. When the war ended, Beard returned to New York City and immersed himself in the cooking community. During this time, he wrote several cookbooks and in 1946 appeared on the first-ever televised cooking show, *I Love to Cook* on NBC. Beard also wrote for national magazines, consulted with restaurant owners and food producers, and owned his own restaurant on Nantucket called Chez Lucky Pierre. By 1954 he was well-known for his efforts to place American cuisine at the front of global cooking styles. The *New York Times* gave him the honorary title of Dean of American Cookery.

In 1955 he opened the James Beard Cooking School and taught there for the next thirty years. He also traveled extensively, promoting good-quality American food to a nation just waking up to its own unique culinary heritage. Over his lifetime, Beard wrote twenty-six cookbooks and many magazine articles and columns. He was tireless in his work as a mentor to America's young chefs and cookbook writers. Beard died in 1985, but his name will forever be linked with quality American cuisine.

The James Beard Foundation Awards were first given out in 1991. The awards are often called the Oscars of the Food World. The foundation gives out annual awards for excellence in many categories including Rising Star Chef of the Year, Best New Restaurant, and Lifetime Achievement for a career that has impacted food in America.

Seasoned Profile

Name: Allen Routt
Job: Owner and chef, The Painted Lady, Newburg, Oregon

When did you discover a love for food and want to focus your career in the culinary arts?

I was born and raised in Roanoke, Virginia. We were the typical middle-class family: both parents worked and my oldest brother watched out for us after school. I was the fourth of five boys. We had a lot of freedom to run and play. As a kid I liked to play restaurant games. My grandma cooked a lot, and I loved being with her on the farm. She cooked from scratch and grew what she could in her garden. My other grandma lived in Florida. When we went to see her, we got to eat fresh fruits like oranges, mangos, papaya, and grapes. I remember how much I loved the smell of orange oil on my skin.

I struggled in public school and felt that I wasn't taught much; I wasn't challenged. I knew early on that a four-year college wasn't for me. One day as I was driving down Franklin Road, I saw a sign on a Mexican restaurant that said they were looking for a line cook. I didn't know anything about working in a kitchen, but the owner hired me anyway. It was physically and mentally challenging, but rewarding because I was part of a community.

Walk us through your early culinary journey, your education and work experience.

The Mexican restaurant had joint parking with a high-end Brazilian restaurant owned by a man named José Santos. When I was seventeen, maybe eighteen, he hired me and taught me all about food preparation. By watching him, I learned what it means to be the owner of a restaurant and the choices that have to be made. Santos saw potential in me and suggested that I go to the Culinary Institute of America (CIA), but only if I was serious about becoming a chef.

At the time I was looking for something I could invest my life in, commit to. I saw culinary school as a way to open doors and give me a chance to travel. I applied when I was nineteen and, with a letter of recommendation from Santos,

I was accepted. I went to CIA for a while and then had an externship in San Francisco. I worked for Bradley Ogden while he was opening his restaurant, One Market, downtown. The quality and sheer variety of product Bradley was bringing into the kitchen every day boggled my mind. I was there for six months and then went back to CIA to finish school.

When did you first decide that you wanted to own your own restaurant?

When I was young, I'd drag my parents off to vacant buildings and try to convince them that it would be a great place to open a restaurant. After I graduated from CIA, I went to work at a restaurant in Washington, Virginia, a small town of about two hundred that is sixty-six miles from the DC area. Today, that small town has one of the world's best restaurants, The Inn at Little Washington. It's owned by Chef Patrick O'Connell. Patrick was a nurturing mentor and under his tutelage, I learned a lot about working in the kitchen and owning a restaurant. He taught me the importance of doing my personal best, to never compromise and to give the customer the very best you can give. While I was working there, I knew I wanted to have a restaurant of my own one day.

What went into your decision to open a restaurant and why did you choose Newburg, Oregon?

After working for Patrick, I restaurant hopped. I had a goal of working under five top chefs who had earned a James Beard award. That goal wasn't reached, but I did work under several really great chefs. I experienced the culinary revolution in southern Florida in the early 2000s. I helped open a restaurant called Mark's in South Beach. That's where I met my wife.

After two years in Florida, we decided to go to the Napa Valley to round out my culinary experiences. From there we moved to Las Vegas where, like in South Beach, a lot of the James Beard award winners were starting restaurants and money was flowing into the town. Talent from around the country was heading there. I worked at the Renoir restaurant and really enjoyed the Las Vegas culinary community.

We didn't stay in Las Vegas long. In early 2004, we took a weekend off and visited Oregon, my wife's home state. We traveled around, visited area restaurants, absorbing the community. We saw potential in Newburg: great people, great wineries, and an all-around great place to build a future. On a more practical note, we saw that Newberg had the demographics to support this kind of restaurant. We studied the topography. It was close to Portland and the state capital of Salem. The town had growth and development potential, along with becoming a Portland bedroom community. It was in the right spot to keep its own identity, the wineries were here, and the bed and breakfasts in the area were gaining national recognition. There's a college in town, as well as a huge hotel and spa. Newburg is becoming a destination and that means customers.

Tell about the process you went through to get The Painted Lady up and running.

Once we were back in Las Vegas, we contacted a real estate agent and set about looking for the perfect place. Eventually we found this 1894 Victorian house. The name comes from San Francisco and its rows of iconic, brightly painted houses. The houses were originally painted in drab colors, using paint leftover from World War II. In the 1960s, artists began to paint them bright colors, and they earned the name painted ladies. The houses helped shape our philosophy for this restaurant: take something old that has great craftsmanship and add a flourish of contemporary expression.

The house needed some work, but it was zoned for commercial use. We worked with the city on fire safety, capacity issues, the installation of a commercial kitchen, and traffic problems. Nothing too unusual. We opened in 2005 and added a guesthouse in 2006.

What advice would you give a young person who is interested in becoming a chef and eventually owning a restaurant?

Learn the basics; learn the techniques; learn discipline. Get some experience. Take any job in the industry, work for a year, and experience the culture. Then stop and think about it. Decide whether or not you liked it; really know that this is what you want to do. This is a career with a lot of different faces. You make it what you need. You have to discover where your soul resides.

THE TALES OF THE TOQUE

You may not know the word, but you know what a toque is: it's the unique hat that most chefs wear. Stories about the origin of the toque abound, and it's almost impossible to nail any one of them down to a single source. Maybe that's what makes it fun, and part of the reason chefs around the world cling to the tradition of wearing one.

Story #1

In the tenth to fifth centuries BC in ancient Assyria, it was common for rulers and prominent leaders to be assassinated by poisoning. Because of this threat, chefs were carefully chosen and highly valued. They were elevated to very high ranks at the court of the king. Because of that rank, they were allowed to wear a cloth "crown." The ribs of these early headdresses were sewed in and later stiffened with starch, and over time became the pleats of the toque.

Story #2

By the end of the sixth century AD, the Byzantine Empire was in decline, and many of the chefs fled to monasteries to escape the invading barbarians from the north. They wore black hats and robes in order to blend in with the monks. Eventually they reclaimed their position in kitchen and began wearing white hats instead of black ones—the toque was born.

Story #3

One day in the early sixteenth century, King Henry the VIII of England found a hair in his supper. The chef was blamed, and the king ordered him to be executed—off with his head! The next chef to the king happily wore a hat, or toque, every time he entered the kitchen.

No matter where the idea for a specific type of hat for a chef came from, the word *toque* was originally defined as a head covering worn by men and women. In the seventeenth century, French toques looked like flattened berets, Italian toques were of medium height and pleated, and the Germans wore ones that were softly gathered and droopy. Other chefs wore skull caps, stocking caps, and even pointed hats with tassels. The neat, tall, stiff, white hat favored by the famous chef Auguste Escoffier and called a *toque blanche* is still worn today. However, the toque is falling out of favor with younger American chefs.

Chef vs. Cook

A chef is a trained professional and the boss of the kitchen. They often hold degrees and certifications. A cook is trained to prepare dishes created by the head chef or sous chef. They have little authority in the kitchen. You don't need to take classes or go to culinary school to be a cook.

The Toque's Pleats

One myth about the toque says that the one hundred pleats signified the number of ways a chef could prepare an egg. Royal chefs boasted that they could prepare an egg in 365 different ways, never serving them the same way twice throughout the year. Today the number of pleats (not one hundred) and the height of the hat are significant. They change as a person rises in rank. A small, unpleated hat is worn by the kitchen staff while a densely pleated hat is only worn by a master chef.

Note:

1. Carter, Sylvia. "Chef Breaks Code to Ancient Recipes: Babylonian Collection Now the Oldest Known to Man." *Los Angeles Times*. 23 May 1985. http://articles.latimes.com/1985-05-23/food/ fo-8362_1_ancient-recipes.

5

The Chef de Partie, the Engine of the Kitchen

No executive chef or sous chef can get the job done without the help of additional kitchen staff. The people who help the most are the chefs de partie, also known as station cooks or line cooks. As a chef de partie, you are on the forefront of the battle to get a meal out of the kitchen at the perfect temperature, at the perfect time, and looking perfect. Your job is stressful, complicated, repetitive, and always hot . . . very, very hot. As mentioned earlier, sometimes a kitchen's temperature can reach well over 130 degrees. And that doesn't include the emotional temperature of the head chef.

As a chef de partie, you are responsible for a specific area of the kitchen, called a station. You work at your station throughout an entire shift and usually remain there for many weeks or months. Cooks become attached to their stations. It is their personal space. Disturbing anything at another cook's station can lead to trouble, and you quickly learn to leave it alone. Every restaurant defines a chef de partie's station responsibilities according to its unique menu requirements. Mastering each station is critical to moving up in the kitchen ranks.

From the moment you walk into the kitchen, your duty as station cook is to focus on the menu of the day and the items you are expected to prepare. You stock your station with everything needed to make assigned dishes as fast and efficiently as possible. In professional kitchens, this is called *mise en place*, a French phrase meaning "everything in place." When the executive chef yells out the first order, you spin into high gear. You work for hours, creating perfect dishes until the last customers have laid down their forks and surrendered in gastronomical delight.

Station cooks are craftsmen who hone their skills over a lifetime. You must constantly adapt to new dishes, perfectly reproducing them fifty to sixty times a night, taking into account the taste, texture, and visual appeal of each plate. You must also coordinate your efforts with other station cooks so that your dish is ready at the same time as every other dish heading for a given table. A station cook usually puts in a twelve- to fourteen-hour day.

GEORGES AUGUSTE ESCOFFIER (1846–1935)

Georges Auguste Escoffier was a leader in the development of modern French cuisine. As France's greatest chef in the early twentieth century, he was responsible for elevating cooking from a mere job to a respected profession. He did this by demanding that his kitchen be organized and that his workers be disciplined team players. He developed the brigade de cuisine, or brigade system, where kitchen responsibilities were divided into stations and each station was run by a chef de partie. This system is still used in many restaurants around the world.

The Brigade System

Much like the military is broken into ranks, the responsibilities in large restaurants are broken down by station. The cook in charge at any station has specific duties to perform. Sometimes these positions are combined, depending on the specific needs of the executive chef. Here are the most common stations and what they prepare.

Patissier (pastry cook): Prepares desserts, candies, petits fours, and baked goods

Confiseur (confectioner): Creates petits fours and candy

Glacier (ice cream maker): Handles any dessert that is cold or frozen

Boulanger (baker): Handles all the breads, pastries, and cakes

Decorateur (decorator): Creates specialty cakes and more ornate desserts, possibly even sugar and chocolate sculpting

Saucier (sauté cook): Prepares hors d'oeuvers, stews, sauces, and sautéed dishes

Poissonnier (fish cook): Prepares fish dishes, including purchasing and cleaning the fish

Rotisseur (roast cook): Prepares meats like roasts, steaks, veal, and lamb, including accompanying sauces

Grillardin (grill cook): Prepares all grilled food

Friturier (fry cook): Prepares all fried foods

Entremetier (vegetable cook): Prepares hot appetizers, soups, vegetables, pastas, and other starches

Potagere (soup cook): Prepares soups (in large kitchens)

Legumier (vegetable cook): Prepares vegetable dishes (in large kitchens)

Garde Manger (pantry cook): Prepares cold foods like salads, cold appetizers, sandwiches, and pâtés

Tournants (wing cook): Fills in where needed at any station

Boucher (butcher): Prepares meats, poultry, and fish before they are delivered to a station

Sprouting Profile

Name: Eli Knauer
Age: 11
Hometown: Baltimore, Maryland
Job (when not studying!): Food critic, Adventures of a Koodie

When did you discover a love for food and want to focus your energy in that area?
I discovered my love for food when I was on a trip to Canada. My mom suggested that I write a blog, so I did!

Why is your blog titled Adventures of a Koodie? What types of restaurants do you focus on?
My food blog is called Adventures of a Koodie because a Koodie is a kid foodie, and a foodie is someone who really likes food. I focus on kid-friendly restaurants and places with good food—sometimes they are both!

What do you do when you don't like a restaurant or some of its food?
I either don't eat it or give it to someone else, like my brother or mother.

How do you balance schoolwork and blogging?
I focus on schoolwork on Mondays through Fridays, and only blog on Saturdays and Sundays. I also blog anytime I'm out of school, like holidays and during the summer.

If you could go anywhere in the world and blog about the restaurants there, where would you go and why?
I would go to Italy because I love Italian food, especially pizza!

Where do you see yourself in ten years?
I see myself in college, earning a degree in food science.

Who has helped you most on your journey and how did he/she help you?
My mom has helped me most because she's the one who has, and still does, edit my posts.

■ ■

A Day in the Life of One Chef de Partie

2:00 PM   Arrive in the locker room, grab some whites and towels, and head to the kitchen. Greet the prep cooks and claim some table space to make some pasta. Get it made, cut, rolled, and blanched before the regular shift begins.

3:00 PM   Set up a line, pull proteins, and finish prep work.

4:15 PM   Finish *mise en place*. Gather sauté pans, sanitation buckets, and trash cans. Fill bottles with wine and oil. Peel and thinly slice garlic, chop parsley and chives, reduce sauces, and cut butter.

5:00 PM   Time to shine! The printer begins to spit out tickets.

5:15 PM   The kitchen gets very busy. Appetizers and salads fly out the door. Word comes that there's already a waiting list. It's going to be a busy night. Pressure builds. The entrée tickets are about to come in.

5:40 PM   The printer is silent. For a moment, there's silence in the kitchen. The first ticket rolls in, and the chef begins to yell out dishes.

7:00 PM   The noise levels rises; the printer continues to chatter. Everyone is in the zone. You know what to do and you do it.

8:00 PM   Almost two hundred people served so far. The printer continues to spit out tickets.

10:30 PM   The number of tickets coming through slows. Time to restock the station, drink some water, go to the bathroom.

11:30 PM   The after-show crowd descends on the restaurant, and the kitchen is roaring again.

1:00 AM	Seating has stopped. Time to clean, sweep, and put everything away. Over four hundred meals served.
2:00 AM	Shift ends. The kitchen is clean. With throbbing feet, it's time to go home.

Sprouting **Profile**

Name: Dominick Cura
Age: 13
Hometown: Seattle, Washington
Job (when not studying!): owner, Eternally Gluten Free website; author, *Eternally Gluten-Free: A Cookbook of Sweets and Inspiration from a Teen!*

You were diagnosed with celiac disease when you were nine. Explain that disease and how it changed your life.

Celiac disease is an autoimmune disorder where the body thinks gluten is something bad. The gluten tricks the body into attacking the villi, the little hairs in the intestine that get nutrients. The person with celiac disease, who continues to eat gluten, will get sick and can suffer from a variety of symptoms.

For me it was shocking to find out that most of the foods I had been eating for the past nine years of my life I'd never be able to eat again. At first it was really hard. I remember going out with my parents to the mall, and we did not know what I could safely eat. My parents would let me have ice cream for lunch. At first when I would go to a friend's house, I would bring my own food and, for birthday parties, my own dessert. Luckily, now my friends and their parents always make sure they have something for me. Going out to dinner or going on vacation with my family required research. My mom would research restaurants where we planned to visit so we would know ahead of time where I could eat. After I was diagnosed, I discovered new foods like quinoa pasta, which I happen to like more than regular pasta. I then started looking past the negative part of having celiac and focusing on the positive. I started my blog so I could share stuff about living gluten-free, like suggesting new products. Over time I made my blog bigger and started baking and sharing my own recipes. Then last April I self-published my gluten-free cookbook.

You developed a website, eternallyglutenfree.com. What prompted you to start it?
I wanted to help people with celiac disease and show them that it's not as bad as they think, especially if they find the good things in it. My gastroenterologist also encouraged me and started telling other patients about it. I was really happy helping people!

You have a cookbook, *Eternally Gluten-Free*. How did that book get started?
My book got started in 2011. I really felt happy living with celiac disease and felt that if I hadn't been diagnosed, my life wouldn't be as good! I found a gluten-free cookbook and started baking from it. Once I ran out of recipes, I decided to start my own recipes. I wanted to inspire people and show them it wasn't that bad to live with celiac disease. So I got the idea of writing a cookbook of dessert recipes. The book also contains a short story of my life and how I turned a negative into a positive.

How do you create new recipes?
It depends what I make. If it's something hard like croissants

or pretzels, I start by looking up the wheat version and then experiment. If it's not a complicated food, I just go for it and write what I think I should use for the recipe, and then I start and change it around while I'm baking. When it doesn't turn out good, I just try it again another day until it is perfect!

Tell about the process you went through in writing your book.

I started by writing my story and baking. I'd just write random parts of my story, and then after tons of editing, it came out to how it is now. After the writing process, it took a while to make sure it was all good. I then sent it in to get reviewed for any major mistakes by the self-publishing company CreateSpace. They checked for specific formatting; once the formatting was correct, it was ready to be self-published. By the way, I'm currently writing a book proposal to send to an editor, and then if it's good, I can work with them to get it published.

How do you balance school work with blogging and creating recipes?

Most of my writing for the book was done before school since I wake up early, at 6:00 AM. I'd wake up early because I could actually do stuff without lots of noise. For the recipes, I'd write the recipe in the morning, and after school I'd bake if I had time. School started again about two months ago, and I haven't had as much time. My posts on my blog have been slowing down, but I usually get it done on the weekend because I know it's really important even if it means getting really stressed about homework.

Can you offer any advice to kids who are thinking about starting a blog or writing a cookbook?

If you want to do either, you need to motivate yourself and really be committed to it. That way, when there are hard times in it (which there will be), you won't give up. If you really are motivated, then go ahead and be creative!

Where do you see yourself in ten years?

Hmm, it's weird to think I'll be twenty-three. . . . Actually, I don't see myself as a baker or a writer. I see myself as a movie director. Also to make sure that comes true, I am working on a documentary about celiac disease. Some of my friends and I make minimovies together, and I've learned lots of stuff from that already. I also see myself helping people, especially those with celiac disease, and maybe holding fund-raisers.

Who has helped you most on your journey and how?

Definitely my mom. She helped me with everything after writing the book. She helped me promote it, get it into stores, get interviewed on blogs, and more. I know if my mom hadn't helped me, my book wouldn't be good at all.

Describe your perfect meal.

Assuming all this is gluten free: Small dinner of lasagna with plenty of ricotta cheese served with a baguette. I'd make sure to have enough room for plenty of dessert, two cream puffs, a big Danish pastry, and a sugar croissant.

Dominick Cura's Recipe
Struffoli

YIELDS 10 SERVINGS

An Italian dessert served at Christmastime, struffoli are little balls of dough that are fried, dipped in honey, piled into a dome, and topped with colorful sprinkles.

3/4 teaspoon xanthan gum
1 cup brown rice flour
1 cup white rice flour
1/4 cup sugar
1/4 teaspoon salt

4 tablespoons butter, sliced into little pieces

3 eggs

Zest from half a lemon

Zest from half an orange

1 1/2 tablespoons white cooking wine

Vegetable oil for frying

1 1/2 cups honey

1/4 cup sugar

Colorful sprinkles

1. Put the xanthan gum, brown rice flour, white rice flour, sugar, and salt in a bowl.
2. Add the butter and mix it with two forks to get big crumbs.
3. Add the eggs, lemon and orange zest, and white wine.
4. Mix until it is doughy. If it is too dry, you can add a little more white wine.
5. Roll the dough into small balls the size of marbles.
6. Pour enough oil in a large saucepan to fill it halfway.
7. Heat over medium-high heat. The oil will be ready when you press the bottom of a wooden spoon against the bottom of the pan and bubbles come out (a trick I learned from my grandmother).
8. Fry the struffoli until golden brown.
9. Combine the honey and sugar in a saucepan over medium-high heat until the sugar is dissolved.
10. Pour the struffoli in and coat the struffoli in the honey.
11. Place on a plate, form into a dome, and top with sprinkles.

Other Positions in the Kitchen

Prep cooks are important in every professional kitchen. When the delivery truck arrives with produce, they help unload it and inspect the contents to make sure it all meets the restaurant's standards. They must know how to work every appliance in the kitchen and keep them maintained. Prep cooks wash, peel, and chop vegetables. They make salads and help with soups, side dishes, and baked goods. Sometimes they help the waitstaff bring food out to the tables. They store leftovers at the end of the day and help clean up the kitchen. Prep cooks do not actually cook. As newcomers to the culinary business, they learn the intricate workings of a kitchen and if they work hard, can start to climb the culinary ladder.

Commis is the French word for "assistant" and refers to a person who is working under a chef de partie as an apprentice. Often a commis is someone who is fresh out of culinary school and in the process of learning the responsibilities of various stations in the kitchen. A commis is also responsible for maintaining station tools, making sure that they are ready at the beginning of a shift and that they are cleaned and put away at the end of the day.

Students working externships may be in the kitchen because people in culinary school are required to have an externship, which is similar to a short-term apprenticeship. Before they graduate, they must go into a professional kitchen, observe, and learn. Although they are often given the drudge work, it's an excellent way to see what it's like to work in a kitchen. Externships are a good way to show the executive and sous chefs that you know how to work hard. Sometimes it opens the door to future employment.

Sprouting Profile

Name: David Pines
Age: 12
Hometown: New York, New York
Job (when not studying!): Food critic, Pines Picks; author, *Pines Picks: A Kid's Guide to the Best Things to Eat and Drink in New York City*

When did you discover a love for food and want to focus your energy in that area?
I must have been really young because I don't remember a time when I didn't love food and trying new restaurants.

As a food critic and author, what does an average day look like for you?
I have a full day of school and then I do sports. In between I always try to get an interesting snack. On the weekends and during vacation times, I have much more time to explore the food scene.

How do you juggle both work and school?
I work hard, and I play hard. For me, trying new food places is very relaxing, and I really look forward to it.

How did you come up with the idea for Pines Picks? How did you choose the restaurants?
I couldn't find a guide that listed all of my favorite foods and places to eat. I decided it made sense to come up with my own guide. I chose the restaurants by getting recommendations from friends. I did tons of research, some on the web and some by having relatives take me around the city to explore different neighborhoods.

Can you offer some tips to kids who are interested in writing a book or a blog?
Go for it, but narrow down what you want to write about before you start and learn to take detailed notes, so you can use them when you write.

How do you handle writing about a restaurant if you don't like the food?
I don't write negative things; I just don't say anything about a restaurant I don't like.

Where do you see yourself in ten years?
I hope to have a dual career as a professional food critic and a professional tennis player, but who knows? Maybe I will open my own restaurant.

Who has helped you most on your journey and how?
My parents have been super supportive, and I have a terrific
publishing assistant.

What is your favorite cooking tool and why?
Nothing beats a really high-quality knife. It helps you cut
up all your ingredients into the perfect size.

Describe your perfect meal.
I can think of many possibilities for a perfect meal.
Here is one that is making me hungry just thinking
about it. For an appetizer, some spicy buffalo wings
with blue cheese dressing and some mozzarella sticks
paired with marinara sauce. For a main course, fresh
pasta with a really good tomato sauce and diced fresh
mozzarella, and some thin-crust cheese pizza. For
dessert, fresh fruit and some hot, gooey, just-out-of-
the-oven chocolate chip or peanut butter chocolate
chip cookies with ice cream.

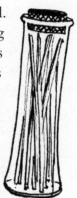

JULIA CHILD: AMERICA'S GRANDE DAME OF COOKING

Julia McWilliams was born in Pasadena, California, in the
summer of 1912. She attended the elite Katherine Branson
School for Girls in San Francisco. After high school she
attended Smith College in Massachusetts. She graduated in
1934 with a degree in history and hoped to start a career as
a novelist.

When World War II broke out, she moved to Washington, DC, and volunteered to work for the Office of
Strategic Services, an intelligence agency. As a research
assistant, she and her colleagues traveled around the world

on various assignments. While abroad she met Paul Child, and when the war ended, they returned to the United States and were married.

In 1948 Paul Child was assigned to the American Embassy in Paris. While her husband worked, Julia studied French cooking and took courses at the world-famous Cordon Bleu cooking school. When Simone Beck and Louisette Bertholle asked her to help them write an American cookbook, she eagerly agreed. Their work became a two-volume cookbook, *Mastering the Art of French Cooking*, which was eventually published in 1961. The cookbook was a bestseller for five years and remains popular today.

When Julia appeared on public television to promote her cookbook, the viewing audience loved her. She was smart, sassy, and very funny. That response made her a local celebrity and led to an offer to host her own show, *The French Chef*. Eventually *The French Chef* was syndicated to ninety-six stations. It earned Julia a 1964 George Foster Peabody Award and a 1966 Emmy Award. In the '70s and '80s, she was a regular on *Good Morning America* on ABC. Julia's cookbooks and her television appearances helped change the way Americans relate to their food.

Among her many accomplishments, Julia hosted several other television shows and wrote cookbooks on a number of culinary topics. Throughout her lifetime she received over forty-five awards. In 1993, in recognition of her tireless work to promote excellence in cooking, she became the first woman to be inducted into the Culinary Institute Hall of Fame. In 2000 she received the coveted Légion d'Honneur, France's highest culinary honor. Julia's kitchen, where she cooked for forty years, has been painstakingly moved to the Smithsonian Institute in Washington, DC, where it remains on display for culinary lovers from around the world to see. Julia died in 2004, two days shy of her ninety-second birthday.

The Pastry Chef, the Sweet Side of Cooking

When you think of cooking, does your mind immediately turn to desserts? Do you delight in making pastries or pies that wow everyone who tastes them? Do you look for new and exciting ways to make edible decorations for your cakes? If so, then maybe a career as a pastry chef is right for you.

As a pastry chef, you become the most beloved in the culinary field. You are the one who offers up flaky croissants, elegant éclairs, creamy souffles, and beautifully decorated cakes. Besides these tasty treats, you also learn how to bake breads, muffins, and biscuits. Pastry chefs spend a lot of time researching and taste testing new recipes. Like a sous chef, you spend most of your time in the kitchen—not slaving over a hot stove but slaving over a hot oven. To succeed you need to be organized, detail-oriented, creative, and above all, patient. Besides standing on your feet all day, a creator of culinary confections must be an early riser, sometimes going to work in the wee hours of the morning.

Trends in Baking and Cooking

Mini is in! Creating items in miniature meets the demand for smaller portions and allows each person to choose their own dessert.

Keep it simple. Present clean, fresh foods that are prepared using quality, natural ingredients. Overwhelming the taste buds is out. Clean, comfortable flavors are in.

Buy local. Consumers want to know where their food and the ingredients come from. Organic is not out, but it's taking a backseat to buying from local producers.

Explore specialty diets. The demand for food that is free of dairy, gluten, fat, nuts, and other ingredients is growing.

Stay comfy. The trend is toward foods that hearken back to a simpler time. Flavorful soups and stews, simple vegetables, and homemade fruit pies are some of these.

A Day in the Life of One Pastry Chef

7:00 AM   Stop at the farmers' market. Pick up orders placed the day before: blueberries, strawberries, cherries, and any other good-looking fruit.

8:00 AM   Arrive at work. Check the pantry and write up a list of regular menu items needed for the day.

8:30 AM   Start the yeast bread dough: mixing, rising, proofing, kneading, resting. It all takes time.

9:00 AM   Mix and bake sweet breads, muffins, and biscuits. Jot down ideas for new desserts. Place orders for dry goods and other supplies. Double-check work schedules and fix any problems.

11:00 AM   It's thirty minutes until lunch service begins. Prepare caramel, orange, and mint sauces. Whip the cream. Watch the bread. Start preparing the cake batter.

11:30 AM   Lunch begins. Prepare dessert orders and make sure they go out looking perfect.

1:30 PM   Service settles down. Grab a bite to eat. Meet with the executive chef. Review the fruits that came in. Determine the evening dessert menu.

2:00 PM   Team arrives. Discuss the specialty desserts planned for the evening. Divide up responsibilities, making sure that every detail of every dessert is assigned to someone.

2:30–5:30 PM   Supervise dessert prep, answer questions, and play with new recipes. Make sure garnishes and sauces are ready for every dessert.

What Pastry Chefs Create

- Cakes
- Candies
- Chocolates
- Cookies
- Custards
- Glazes
- Fillings
- Frostings
- Hot and cold desserts
- Ice creams
- Jellies
- Mousses
- Petits fours
- Sorbets
- Tortes

5:30 PM	Dinner begins. Check to see that the desserts are plated and garnished correctly; talk to the pastry cooks and make sure they have what they need to get through the evening.
6:00 PM	It's time to go home!

Name: Ron Ben-Israel

Job: Chef and owner, Ron Ben-Israel Cakes, New York City, New York

Honors: Host of the reality cooking show *Sweet Genius* on Food Network. Seen on *Oprah, Martha Stewart Living,* and other television shows; featured in many national bride and wedding magazines and books, including *Vera Wang on Weddings,* as well as general publications such as *O, the Oprah Magazine, Town and Country,* and the *New York Times,* which called him "the Manolo Blahnik of wedding cakes"; Zagat named him "the wedding cake master."

When did you first decide to focus your career in the culinary arts?

About fifteen years ago, after retiring from my dance career. I attempted many jobs and directions to make a living in

New York City, and making people happy through food seemed to be a natural venue for me.

What education/work path did you take to get where you are today?

I attended four years of a fine arts school, which gave me the eye and skills for design. But everything else I've practiced since has proved helpful in making cakes—my dance career gave me discipline and the attention to details. Even my military service in Israel has helped me through many challenges. I also went to France and apprenticed in Cannes, Beaujolais, and Lyons.

It's important to concentrate on the tasks at hand, and that's what I've done from the beginning. I'm embarrassed with titles and accolades and would rather spend time at the bakery, solving design challenges and coming up with technique solutions.

Who has helped you most on your culinary journey and how?

I'll be always grateful to Betty Van Norstrand, a distinguished cake artist who introduced me to the art of making flowers and decorations out of sugar.

Describe the process that led to your decision to open Ron Ben-Israel Cakes.

It wasn't a hard decision. People started to order my cakes, and I needed to find a place to bake them. I started out renting a nightly kitchen space from a caterer. In the kitchen, I practiced as much as possible. I didn't even choose a business name! Now I'm stuck with my own name on the door. I'm very lucky. I get paid to do what I love!

Your charity of choice is City Harvest. How did you get connected with it, and why is it important to you?

I started donating leftover cakes to City Harvest and became fascinated with their mission and how they operate. Their people are so devoted to the cause of hunger. I'm honored to be a part of the organization. Since I supply a luxury item, working with the hungry brings balance into my world.

Tell me how you got started teaching, what you like most about teaching, and what you expect from your students.

Like everything else in my career, I didn't intend to teach. I couldn't find employees who had the skills necessary to carry out my visions. So I started training them myself. A lot of the candidates came from the International Culinary Center (founded as the French Culinary Institute). Over time I gravitated toward that school. I wanted to train future pastry chefs in an institution that was already providing them with an excellent education.

What advice would you give a young person who might be interested in becoming a cake designer?

Find a good instructor/mentor to get you started and then practice, practice, practice.

What do you see as future trends in your part of the culinary industry?

Oh, I think designer cakes will keep on developing and growing in their daring and beauty. We will always have the classical techniques, but newer ways will be discovered and will allow us to achieve greater feats of fancy.

Describe your perfect meal.

Simple: My perfect meal would be whatever Chef Dan Barber, at Blue Hill Restaurant in New York, has created from fresh, farm ingredients that day!

MARCUS GAVIUS APICIUS—AN ANCIENT AND FLAMBOYANT GOURMET

Marcus Gavius Apicius lived in the first century AD, during the reign of Emperor Tiberius. He was a very wealthy man whose home was somewhere near modern-day Naples, Italy.

Apicius tried to live the most lavish lifestyle possible. To that end, he entertained his guests by creating and serving the strangest dishes possible. His reckless spending was fuel for gossip among many members of society, especially the lords and ladies who willingly partook of his unusual, exotic, and sometimes dangerous meals. He created dishes like jellyfish omelets, flamingo tongue, boiled parrot, and stuffed mouse.

Apicius loved the attention his meals brought and spent his entire fortune creating them. When he realized that his money was almost gone, he invited everyone to a huge feast. When it was over, he quietly poisoned himself to death.

An ancient cookbook, *De Re Coquinaria*, or *The Art of Cooking*, is attributed to him. However, the book was compiled in the late fourth and early fifth centuries and only about three-fifths of the recipes are Apicius's own creations.

Specialty Careers for Pastry Chefs

Bakers

Bakers focus their careers on yeast breads, quick breads, muffins, and other bread products. Often they open their own bakeries and sell to the public, to small specialty stores, or to local grocery outlets. Within that career, some may choose to specialize in specific markets.

Artisan breads are crafted in small batches using few ingredients and no preservatives or chemicals. Examples of artisan breads include the country French loaf, whole-grain farm-style bread, and stone-ground wheat bread. Artisan breads have a short shelf life and should be eaten within a few days.

Gluten-free products are produced in bakeries that have been cleansed of all traces of wheat and gluten. Bakers use various ingredients like almond flour, rice flour, and potato starch to create their own unique flour blend. With the increase in demand for gluten-free foods, these foods' tastes and textures are almost equal to their wheat counterparts.

Kosher products conform to Jewish dietary laws. Bakeries can be certified by a Kosher certifying agency whose requirements can range from liberal to very conservative.

Boutique desserts are cute or clever and trendy. One example of this is cupcakes. Stores and television shows devoted to the cupcake are very popular. Bakers who specialize in cupcakes focus on bringing unique flavor combinations and designs to their customers. These cupcakes can be used for events ranging from a child's birthday party to a formal wedding. Cookies can also be boutique desserts. They are a staple in most bakeries. For a baker to specialize in them, that person must create new and unique flavors. Usually the artistic side to this specialty rests in the cut-outs and decorations.

Ethnic desserts include Italian cannoli, Middle Eastern baklava, Japanese mochi-based sweets, and Latin American *pastel de tres leches*.

Dairy-free desserts are baked in facilities that are cleansed of all dairy products. Bakers replace dairy by using alternatives to milk like liquid extracted from coconuts, almonds, or hazelnuts. Dairy-free bakeries may also create products that are nut free, gluten free, or vegan.

Name: Phebe Rossi
Job: Founder and baker, Nuflours: A Gluten Free Bakery, Seattle, Washington

Name: Amanda Bedell
Job: Co-owner and marketer, Nuflours: A Gluten Free Bakery, Seattle, Washington

When did you first decide to focus your career on gluten-free products?
Phebe: Good gluten-free products didn't exist back when I went gluten free. I initially developed gluten-free recipes for myself. I was working full-time while baking for friends and acquaintances. I was feeling unfulfilled and realized that I needed to shift my focus and officially open my own business. I was living in Portland, Oregon, at the time. I studied the gluten-free market and decided to move to Seattle. Portland has numerous gluten-free options, but Seattle was a veritable gluten-free desert.
Amanda: I was diagnosed with gluten sensitivity in 2009. About a year later, after struggling to find good food, I seriously dove into changing my career and focusing on opening a gluten-free bakery. Starting my own business had been a dream of mine and a topic of conversations with my friends and family.

History of the Cupcake

1796   The first recipe for "a light cake to bake in small cups" appears in *American Cookery*, the first cookbook written by an American, Amelia Simmons.

1828   The term *cupcake* is used for the first time in Eliza Leslie's cookbook, *Seventy-Five Receipts for Pastry, Cakes, and Sweetmeats*.

1914   Tastykake sells the first snack cake in America. They introduce a two-cake package in 1915 and add a third cupcake for the same price during the Great Depression.

1920s   Frosting is added to cupcakes, usually chocolate or vanilla flavored.

2000s   New York City boutique cupcake shops gain in popularity after being featured on the television show *Sex and the City*.

2005   Sprinkles Cupcakes in Beverly Hills, California, opens the world's first cupcakes-only bakery.

2010   US cupcake sales grew by 11 percent.[1]

2012   Americans consumed 770,000,000 cupcakes.[2]

2012   *Cupcake Wars* on the Food Network reaches 1.6 million viewers.[3]

What education/work path did you take to get where you are today?
Phebe: I grew up on a farm and have been baking my entire life. My college degree is actually in fine arts, so really, I have a well-rounded education for creating beautiful and delicious baked goods!

Amanda: I have a bachelor's degree, with a double major in communications, public relations track, and technical writing. I spent ten years in a variety of public-relations roles in the entertainment and nonprofit industries. My education and work background mean that I can successfully develop the Nuflours brand.

Describe the process that led to the decision to open a gluten-free bakery.

Phebe: It was the next natural step for me. When I first started selling my baked goods, I was baking out of a commissary and selling them at farmers markets, to wholesale accounts, and to individual clients who wanted custom cakes for special events. I wanted to provide my customers with a regular outlet for my baked goods.

Amanda: The idea for Nuflours came out of my need for tasty gluten-free goods. I was unsatisfied with the products available at the time, and began baking and cooking for myself. After feeding friends, family, and coworkers (and receiving lots of praise), the seed was planted: I should start my own business, centered on serving only delicious gluten-free products. The trials I faced while learning to live gluten free were the driving force behind wanting to open a gluten-free bakery. I wanted to be a resource for people. I wanted to share my food, recipes, and knowledge with everyone, so that it's easier for them than it was for me.

How did you meet your business partner?

Amanda: I took a class on how to start a small food business. I learned during that class that the vision I had for Nuflours wasn't a one-person show. I needed a partner, someone who knew how to bake and create recipes. I put out feelers online, sending my request to friends and business contacts, posting inquiries on gluten-free group pages, and reaching out to local culinary schools. An acquaintance in the gluten-free community urged me to reach out to Phebe. I sent her an email within minutes, and the rest is history!

What was it about your business partner that made you say, "I can work with this person; we can successfully run a business together"?
Phebe: Our first meeting lasted five hours! We were both surprised to meet someone who had such a similar business vision and yet a completely different professional background. Our skill sets complement each other. My areas of expertise are in small-business management, product development (recipes!), and artistic creation (fine arts degree). Amanda comes from a public-relations background and has experience with the public aspects of business management like marketing and customer service. It's key in a successful business partnership to define roles and trust each other to carry out those roles.

What are some of the steps you had to take to start your small business?
Amanda: Draft a business agreement. Hire a lawyer to make sure the paperwork is done correctly. Hire an accountant and bookkeeper to ensure that the IRS likes our paperwork too.

Obtain licenses. All of them, including state business license, city business license, food handlers cards, Washington State Department of Agriculture license, city health department license, insurance, and the list goes on.

File our trademark. Our business has a unique (and distinctive!) name.

Search for a location. Our space needed to be large enough to hold a functioning commercial kitchen, including multiple ovens, work benches, refrigerator and freezer, dry ingredients storage, etc., and we needed space for the café including tables, chairs, pastry cases, juice bar, and espresso and tea equipment.

Shop for a lot of equipment, from small wares, like whisks, mixing bowls, and wooden spoons to large convection ovens, a walk-in refrigerator and freezer, and point-of-sale equipment.

Build out. Find good contractors who know building codes, and then build out the space. Keep to deadlines so that we open on schedule.

Hire bakers and baristas. Look for people who are engaged, enjoy what they do, and want to learn.

While doing all that, we also did:

Brand development. We decided on the focus of our brand, all aspects from a logo to the focus of the bakery and how we will interact with our customers. That all aids in the development of café aesthetic and uniforms too. Social media and website development.

Fund-raising, including crowd sourcing and reaching out to individual investors.

What advice would you give a young person who might be interested in starting a bakery/café?
Phebe: Be highly engaged in what you do. (I don't like the phrase "be passionate.")

Research. A business like ours didn't exist in Seattle; we saw an opportunity and ran with it.

Have a business plan, recipes, an idea of what precisely it is you want to do. It's easy to get distracted and sidetracked in the food business!

Don't be afraid to ask questions, especially of other food professionals.

Do as much planning and research as you can before investing too much money.

Be prepared to work harder than you ever have before and anticipate not making money for the first few years until your business is established.

Set short-term goals and celebrate small successes. Creating a business from scratch is a huge undertaking but hugely rewarding—don't forget to congratulate yourself once in a while.

Most of all have fun!

We founded our business for many reasons but mostly because we love feeding people and realized that we're good at it. At the end of the day, we've positively affected people's lives, and that's what matters: feeding people's bodies to feed their souls.

There are days when I go home exhausted. When that happens, I look in the mirror and remind myself that without me, someone wouldn't have a birthday cake. Not the end of the world, I know, but we make the world a happier place!

How do you see social media helping your business?
Amanda: We are using social media to enhance our relationship with our customers. We want to be on their minds, even when they're at home. We'll use social tools to drive our product development, further our brand awareness, and create a sense of community for our customers and local businesses. We believe a strong social media presence will increase sales and help achieve our sales goals.

What do you see as future trends in your part of the culinary industry?
Phebe: Trends are a funny, finicky thing. I see desserts and baked goods trending toward more savory flavors. People are attempting to be more health conscious and to that end are looking for "healthier" options. Desserts are trending to a smaller, European size and going for more potent/decadent flavors. And local, local, local. People want to know where their food comes from.

Describe your perfect meal.
Phebe: I'm such a mood eater, it depends on the season. In the summer I'm happy with gluten-free bruschetta, a

little dish of hummus, and grilled vegetables. In the winter I love oven-roasted kale with a poached egg on top, spinach macaroni and cheese, and pumpkin tarts with shaved chocolate and a dollop of lemon-infused mascarpone whipped cream.

Amanda: I'm a seasonal eater too. In the summer I love salads, fresh cold soups, and lots of fruits. In the winter I tend to crave comfort food like home-cooked, fresh winter vegetable stir-fry with a spicy sauce, spicy three-bean chili, or a nice savory meatloaf. And no matter what the season, a nice, big, rich chocolate brownie is perfect for dessert.

Phebe Rossi's Recipe
Pumpkin Tea Cake

YIELDS 2 LOAVES

215 grams sugar
230 grams pumpkin puree
100 grams canola oil
2 eggs
170 grams flour
1/4 teaspoon xanthan gum
1 teaspoon baking powder
1/2 teaspoon baking soda
1/4 teaspoon kosher salt
1/2 teaspoon cinnamon
1/4 teaspoon nutmeg

1. Heat your oven to 350 degrees Fahrenheit.
2. Oil two loaf pans (9 x 5 "regular" loaf pans).
3. In a medium bowl, blend together sugar, pumpkin, oil, and eggs until smooth.
4. In a separate bowl, gently stir the dry ingredients together until well blended.

5. Add the dry ingredients to the wet blend and mix together until just incorporated. The batter may be a little lumpy, and this is okay!
6. Pour the batter into the prepared pans.
7. Bake for 55 minutes, until a toothpick inserted in the center comes out with just a few moist crumbs.
8. Let the loaves cool in the pans for 10 minutes before removing them and placing them on a cooling rack.

Wedding Cake Designers

Pastry chefs who specialize in wedding cake design can be found in grocery stores with in-house bakeries and independent bakeries, or they can own their own business. This specialty requires an understanding of art, structural design, and engineering. Since wedding cakes come in all shapes, sizes, and designs, the wedding cake designer must be ready for anything. The completed product is an edible work of art, a three-dimensional masterpiece.

Basic Steps to Creating a Wedding Cake

The concept and plan. Meet with the couple and determine the vision for the cake. Things to consider include where the wedding will take place, what time of day, will it be formal or casual, what the colors and theme are, and any other elements of the event. Let the couple taste test various cakes, brainstorm ideas, and look at a portfolio of possible designs.

Bake the cake. Once the elements of the cake are selected, it's time to bake a few sample cakes and form a delivery plan. You'll need ingredients, utensils, bowls, pans, and lots of space and plenty of time to work.

Frosting and filling. When choosing a frosting, there are two basic types: butter cream and fondant. When frosting the cake,

consider the texture, color, and any added elements before starting. The correct choice of frosting could save you hours of work
later on.

Flowers, borders, and other design elements. Here's where
creativity shines. Bringing unique elements to the cake design can
take a wedding cake from ordinary to extraordinary.

Preserve the finished product. Most wedding cakes aren't built
in a day. At each stage, the cake must be properly stored or frozen.

Stages of Cooking Sugar

Making various candies requires precision temperatures for
the sugar. All of the degrees listed are in Fahrenheit.

235–240, soft ball stage:
Used to make fudge, fondant, and pralines

245–250 firm ball stage:
Used to make marshmallows and caramels

250–265, hard ball stage:
Used to make rock candy, gummies, and nougats

270–290, soft crack stage: Used to make butterscotch
and saltwater taffy

300–310, hard crack stage:
Used to make lollipops, toffee, brittles, and hard candy

Over 350, yuck stage:
Useless burned sugar

Assemble the cake. Here's the tricky part. Things to consider are how far the cake has to travel, what the weather conditions are, and what can be assembled in house and what has to wait to be added on site.

Transport the cake. If assembling a cake is tricky, transporting the finished product is downright nerve-racking. Remove any items in the vehicle that could fall onto the cake, take the shortest route or the one with the least number of turns, bring extra frosting and decorations for repairs, and drive slowly.

Confectioners

Confectioners are chefs who specialize in making candy. Whether it's lollipops, cream-filled chocolates, or flavored taffy, the candy chef knows how to make it. Confectioners who become chocolatiers focus their careers in the world of chocolate.

THE HISTORY OF CHOCOLATE

The origin of the word *chocolate* can be traced to the Aztec word *xocoatl*, which refers to a bitter drink brewed from the cacao bean.

> *Cacao* refers to the plant or its beans.
> *Chocolate* refers to anything made from the beans.
> *Cocoa* refers to chocolate in powdered form.

Cacao has been around for over three thousand years. Anthropologists at the University of Pennsylvania discovered cacao in pottery in Honduras that date to 1400 BC. The plant is native to northwestern South America. The beans were valuable enough to be used as currency, and their popularity spread along trade routes. Sometime in the fifth or sixth century AD, the Maya carried the bean to what is now Mexico. Cacao was used as a spice in food and as a

What Kind of Candy Do They Like?

China and other Asian countries: Pickled or preserved fruits covered in a sweet-sour-salty powder, or candied ginger or fruit

Holland, Denmark, and Finland: Strong and salty varieties of black licorice

Central and South America: Thick, very sweet form of caramelized milk called *dulce de leche*

France, Italy, and Spain: Nougat, sometimes made with rosewater and pistachios

Middle East: Turkish Delight, a jellied sweet that is flavored with rosewater or fruit and that can contain almonds, walnuts, hazelnuts, or pistachios; treats made from honey, ground sesame seeds or nuts, and sometimes rosewater and saffron

Indonesia: Chewy, spicy treat made from ginger and potato starch

Brazil: Candy balls made using condensed milk and cocoa powder and then rolled in chocolate sprinkles

Southeast Asia and South America: Candies made from a mixture of chili peppers, salt, sugar, and fruit—often tamarind or mango—tasting tangy, hot, salty, and sweet all at the same time

Japan: Candies made from millet jelly and sweet rice, and then wrapped in a thin sheet of edible rice paper

drink. For the drink, they toasted the beans, ground them up, added the powder to hot water, and then added flavors like maize, vanilla, or chili. It was a drink fit for the emperor and was only consumed by the nobility and priests.

When the Spanish conquistadores arrived, they noticed the benefits of this chocolate drink and used it to stave off hunger when they marched long distances. The Spanish brought the beans to Europe, where they were rejected because of the bitter flavor. Over time, the addition of vanilla, cinnamon, black pepper, and then cane sugar sent chocolate's popularity soaring. When Pope Pius V decided that chocolate could be consumed during required fasting, many Catholic countries embraced the drink.

In the 1600s, chocolate houses opened in Europe. They were social meeting places for the elite, and chocolate became trendy and very expensive. In 1828 a Dutch chemist found a way to separate cacao butter from cacao liquor and created the cocoa powder we recognize today. This discovery moved chocolate from being a beverage of the wealthy to a beverage of the masses. The chocolate-house culture changed and slowly nurtured the democratic political movements of the eighteenth and nineteenth centuries.

In 1847 Joseph Fry discovered that by reintroducing cacao butter back into cocoa, he could make a moldable chocolate paste—the first chocolate bar. Cadbury started making chocolate candy in England in 1868, and milk chocolate appeared a few years later. Today chocolate manufacturing in the United States is a $4 billion industry, and the average American consumes about a half pound of it per month.

Notes:
1. "The Rise of the Cupcake." Ideal Bite. November 2012. http://idealbite.com/the-rise-of-the-cupcake Accessed 13 December 2012.
2. Ibid.
3. "The Rise of the Cupcake." All Culinary Schools. http://www.allculinaryschools.com/culinary-careers/article/the-rise-of-cupcakes Accessed 13 December 2012.

7

Cooking for Many, Cooking for Few

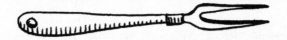

Do you love the idea of cooking food that is the highlight of a party? Are you outgoing, and can you easily chat with lots of different people? Are you comfortable being the one in charge of every last detail of an event? If so, catering may be the culinary career for you.

If you decide that catering is where you want to focus your energy, be prepared to work a variety of occasions. Caterers are used for important family events like birthday parties, anniversary celebrations, and memorial services; for businesses events, like retirement parties, product launches, and holiday celebrations; and for large company events, like movie premiers, corporate conferences, and award ceremonies. No matter the event, the caterer is responsible for everything related to the food service—making the food, getting it to the event, serving it, and cleaning up—and may be responsible for everything about the event.

For larger events, you work closely with an event planner. The event planner is responsible for everything related to the event, including hiring you and making sure you do your job.

For smaller events, the caterer does it all. From the first meeting with the client to decide on a theme until the last pot has been scrubbed and put away, every detail falls on your shoulders. Besides knowing how to cook, being highly organized is the most important skill for any caterer.

Things to Think About Before Starting a Catering Business

A business plan: This includes a business name, an outline of how the business will operate and be managed, financial considerations, and projected profit and loss statements.

A business location: Whether working out of your home or a rented space, check local and state laws, apply for permits and licenses, and consult an insurance agent. The kitchen must be inspected, and you must follow strict cleaning and safety procedures.

Start-up costs: Where will you get the money to start your business? Some costs include permits, licenses, rent, equipment, staff salaries, advertising, living expenses, and product expenses. If you borrow money, you must budget for payments plus interest.

Working with or without help: Working alone is difficult even for small events. Hiring good employees, making payroll, scheduling and tracking work hours, and managing workloads are some of the skills you need when bringing on additional help.

Food choices: What types of food will you focus on? Do you want to specialize in one style of food or be able to meet a variety of client needs?

Rent or buy: How will you get the items you need for your events? Will you work with vendors or own your own tables, chairs, serving equipment, etc.?

Types of Food Service

There are several ways you may be asked to serve food. No matter the style, the dishes you provide must be the same for the first person served as they are for the last person served.

Butler style: Food is served by staff from platters, bowls, or trays. The food is dished out to individual guests so each person can accept or decline each course.

Plated service: Food is arranged on the plate in the kitchen and delivered by staff to each guest.

Family style: Plates and bowls of food are set on each table. The guests serve themselves and pass the food around to others.

Food stations: Food is prepared and guests go to stations—soup stations, children's stations, salad stations, or dessert stations—and choose the food they want.

Buffet style: Food is set on decorated tables. Guests either serve themselves or are given a portion from a server. Using servers helps with portion control and eliminates some waste.

Advertising: How will you advertise your business? From reliance on word of mouth to hiring an agency, the choice starts with a plan. Plan out how you will advertise.

Work schedule: Will you work weekends? How many events will you work in a week? A month? Decide what will work for you, balancing profits with possible burnout.

Name: Scott Ketterman
Job: Chef and owner, Crown Paella, Portland, Oregon

When did you first decide to focus your career in the culinary arts?

My first position in a kitchen was during the summer of 1995. I really loved the work, but it wasn't until three years later that I decided to pursue it as my career path.

What education/work path did you take to get where you are today?

When I made the decision to become a chef, I formed a long-term plan for gaining work experience. I relocated to a city with good restaurants, and then I sought out the chefs who I felt would be good mentors. I accepted low-paying, entry-level positions and worked for no less than one year at each place. After completing that year, I would look for the next restaurant where I would be challenged to grow. This path, ultimately, led me to work in some of the most renowned kitchens in Europe.

You and your wife formed the catering company Crown Paella. Describe the journey you took and

the decisions you had to make when deciding to go into the catering business.

Every success story in this business is one part talent and one part luck. My wife and I were both working for a restaurant/catering company when we made the decision to leave in order to pursue a restaurant of our own. Since I was working as a chef, which meant many seventy-hour workweeks, I knew that I wouldn't have the time to start a new business without first leaving my position. This meant that I would have to find a job with fewer requirements to free up my schedule.

After a few months of watching the want ads, and my final days at the restaurant approaching, we decided to start a small business simply cooking paella for parties. If I booked a few events a month, then I would be able to cover my living expenses and remain flexible.

We set forth with nothing more than a website, business cards, and a prep kitchen, which we rented by the hour. The last detail was to get the word out in order to bring in some business. We used our media and trade contacts to send out a media release, so people would know what we were up to. As quickly as we did that, we started getting a lot of business. We quickly realized that our contingency plan was a viable business that we couldn't turn away from, and we put our energy toward growing the company into a full-service catering business.

You focus on traditional Spanish cooking. Why?

I'm inspired by Spanish food. I've traveled to Spain a number of times and simply love the food. It's an ingredient-driven cuisine, which really resonates well with people. Also, there are no other Spanish caterers in the area, so we have a little competitive edge that way.

Describe the preparation you go through to get ready for and execute a typical event.

Every event is different. Some require months of planning;

others are quite simple. Every event begins with a conversation. We try to determine exactly what our clients are looking for or what they envision. We create proposals and revise as needed until we find the right match. Then we have follow-up meetings to make sure that all the details are covered. Before an event, we do site visits to make sure we're properly prepared for the space and that we have considered everything that we'll need to be successful. Then we arrange for staffing and rentals, source products, prep food, pack equipment and vehicles. When we arrive for an event, there are a lot of details to organize. We basically build a restaurant on location, run service, then tear it all down, take it away, clean it up, and pack everything away for the next event.

Who has helped you most on your culinary journey and how?
Every chef I have ever had the pleasure of working for has helped me along the way. The chefs who have helped me the most are the ones who have pushed me the hardest and expected the most from me.

Do you use social media? If so, how? And in what way is it useful to your business?
Yes. It's a great way to reach people and to get instant feedback. You can really gauge what types of events and food items interest people simply by the number of people who reach out.

What advice would you give a young person who might be interested in starting a catering business?
My advice is to start by working in the field. Go to the most reputable catering businesses and take any position you can get. Always work hard and you'll be rewarded with more responsibility. That's the only way to learn the business. It's a tough business that requires a lot of knowledge and understanding to be successful.

What do you see as future trends in your part of the culinary industry?

There is going to be a lot of growth and focus on quality in this field. The culinary industry is one of the fastest growing industries right now. Consumers are becoming increasingly savvy, and the catering companies that will succeed are the one that keep up with the quality of contemporary restaurants.

Chef Scott Ketterman's Recipe
Golden Chanterelle and Leek Tart with Chèvre

YIELDS 1 TART

Crust
2 1/2 cups all-purpose flour
1 tablespoon sugar
1 teaspoon salt
2/3 cup cold, unsalted butter, cubed
1 egg, lightly beaten
1/4 cup cold water

Filling
2 leeks
2 tablespoons butter
1 1/2 pounds chanterelles, cleaned
2 eggs
1 cup heavy cream
2 teaspoons sherry vinegar
4 tablespoons olive oil
2 ounces fresh chèvre cheese
Salt and pepper

For the Crust
1. Heat oven to 350 degrees Fahrenheit.

2. Combine flour, sugar, salt, and butter in a bowl.
3. Mix until it resembles the texture of oats.
4. Add the egg and water
5. Mix together to just form dough.
6. Cover the dough and refrigerate for 30 minutes.
7. Grease and flour a fluted tart pan.
8. Roll the dough out, line the pan with the dough, and prick the bottom of the tart with a fork.
9. Refrigerate the shell an additional 30 minutes.
10. Line the shell with foil and fill with beans or baking beads.
11. Bake for about 20 minutes.
12. Uncover the tart.
13. Bake for an additional 5 minutes or until crust is lightly browned on the bottom.
14. Cool the shell in the tart pan.

For the Filling
1. Slice the mushrooms into 1/2-inch pieces and sauté in the olive oil in a hot pan over high heat until the mushrooms have released their liquid and become lightly browned.
2. Transfer mushrooms to a bowl, season with salt and pepper, and cool.
3. Trim the dark-green tops from the leeks.
4. Split them lengthwise and rinse with cold water to remove any dirt.
5. Slice the leeks into thin semicircles and sauté in the butter over medium heat until they are soft and translucent.
6. Season with salt and pepper and add to the bowl of mushrooms to cool slightly.

To Assemble
1. Beat together the eggs, heavy cream, sherry vinegar, and salt and pepper to taste.
2. Pour half of the mixture over the mushrooms and leeks.
3. Pour the mushroom mixture into the tart shell and pour the remaining custard over it.

4. Bake until just set, approximately 15 minutes.
5. Remove the tart from the oven.
6. Crumble the chèvre over the top.
7. Return to the oven for 5 minutes longer just to set the cheese.
8. Cool and serve at room temperature or warmed.

■ ■

Basic Responsibilities of a Caterer

- Work well with clients
- Set appropriate prices
- Handle contracts
- Cook large amounts of good food
- Hire and manage waitstaff
- Set up tables, chairs, linens, and flatware
- Serve the food
- Clean up after the event

A Day in the Life of One Caterer

6:30 AM   Get up, make coffee, and eat breakfast.

7:00 AM   Answer emails, do paperwork, check your schedule: a cocktail party tonight and a buffet-style retirement party in three days.

8:00 AM   Get ready to go—you're meeting a client at 8:30.

8:30 AM   Meet with the potential clients to discuss their wedding and show them what services are available. If they ask for a bid, gather further details like event date, time, place, style, number of guests, menu choices, etc.

11:00 AM	Back home. Work on a fiftieth-anniversary dinner menu. Put finishing touches on a contract for a wedding that's six months away. Jot down more organized notes for the new wedding bid. Call the temp agency to confirm the staff for tonight's party and the upcoming retirement party. Go over supply lists for the retirement party.
2:00 PM	Hit the kitchen. Make all the hors d'oeuvres for the cocktail party. There are lots and lots of bite-size finger foods to make, pack, and transport.
6:00 PM	Arrive at the hotel and greet the hotel staff. Carry food and trays into the kitchen. Make sure everything is ready to go.
6:30 PM	Hired staff arrives. Hand out company aprons. Start filling serving trays while giving detailed instructions on how to properly serve the guests.
7:00 PM	Meet with client's event planner for last-minute instructions.
7:30 PM	Guests arrive. Oversee servers and kitchen help.
9:30 PM	Event ends. Clean up the kitchen, pack up trays and leftover food, and carry it all back to the truck. Dismiss staff.
10:30 PM	Arrive home, exhausted.

Making Garnishes

One challenge for any cook is using the right garnish to make a dish as beautiful and as appetizing as possible. Garnishes are made using fruits, vegetables, herbs, chocolate, or anything else that's edible and adds interest to your dishes. Don't forget to use flowers; a lot of them are edible. Be sure that your garnish choice goes with the food you are serving. A chocolate garnish, no matter how beautiful, doesn't belong on a plate of lasagna. Try creating something from a tomato instead. From a simple slice of orange to an intricate fruit bouquet, the possibilities are limited only by your imagination.

Simple Tools You Can Use to Make Garnishes

Apple corer: Cut holes in fruits and vegetables or make them into tubes.

Cookie cutters: Cut softer items, like cheese and marzipan.

Grater: Shave cinnamon, chocolate, and citrus peels.

Garnish Tips

- Blanch vegetables to heighten color.
- Use foods with strong colors, like carrots, radishes, oranges, and bell peppers.
- Store garnishes in an airtight container to keep them from drying out.
- Store dry garnishes in a cool dry place.

Knives: Cut through larger items like fruits and vegetables and make small, fine cuts to create shapes.

Melon baller: Make large, medium, and small balls and half balls.

Scissors: Snip herbs and onions to make clusters and bouquets.

Slicer: Make slices of varying thicknesses.

Strainer: Scatter sugar, powdered sugar, cocoa, or other dry powdery items onto delicate dishes.

Toothpicks and skewers: Hold things together.

Vegetable peeler: Make thin strips or curls.

CHALLENGE
Make a Garnish

You will need:
- One apple
- A knife
- A spoon
- Lemon juice
- A small candle
- Whole cloves
- Cranberries, blueberries, or grapes
- Toothpicks

1. Choose a nicely shaped apple of any color.
2. Slice off the top of the apple.
3. Scoop a hole from the center sized to fit your candle.
4. Coat the exposed apple flesh with lemon juice to prevent it from browning.
5. Press the cloves into the apple, creating a design of your choice.
6. Put one end of a toothpick into a cranberry, blueberry, or grape.
7. Put the other end into the top of the apple, outside the hole you carved.
8. Continue using toothpicked fruit to make a circle around the candle hole.
9. Put the candle into the hole.

Voilà! You have a candle holder that can be used to decorate a dinner table or a buffet table.

Volume Cooks, Serving the Masses

If you are not interested in owning your own business, maybe volume cooking is the place for you. Volume cooks excel at preparing good food for huge numbers of people. The way this is done is determined by the institution you work for. Here's where some volume cooks find work:

- Airlines
- Colleges and universities
- Correctional facilities, like jails and prisons
- Cruise ships
- Hospitals
- Large company cafeterias
- Military bases and schools
- Production kitchens where food is prepared and sent to other institutions
- Nursing and retirement homes
- School cafeterias

Sprouting Profile

Name: Michael Prados
Age: 12
Hometown: Baton Rouge, Louisiana
Job (when not studying!): Food critic
Honors: a White House Healthy Lunchtime Challenge State Winner; attended the first White House Kids' State Dinner

When did you discover a love for food and want to focus your energy in that area?

I have always loved food, since I was a little kid. My first two words were *Iron Chef*!

As a food blogger and critic, where do you get the ideas for your entries?

My family and I go out for food adventures, and I blog a lot about the new places we go. We also like to cook together as a family. We make up new recipes and try different recipes.

How do you juggle both work and school?

It's hard at times, especially with more and more homework as I go up each grade. Somehow I manage to find time for blogging.

Can you offer some tips for writing a successful blog?

Don't take blogging that seriously—just have fun while writing. It's good to describe what you're talking about deeply because it should be something you really enjoy.

Tell us about your visit to the White House for the very first Kids' State Dinner.

I have to say that it was really cool meeting other kids with recipes that were creative, healthy, and delicious. When we got to Washington, DC, they gave us a tour of Julia Child's kitchen and other parts of the Smithsonian. The next day we went to the White House, and I found out that I was going to sit next to Michelle Obama for lunch!

Have you ever gone to a restaurant and not liked the food? How did you review that restaurant?

I would say that the restaurant could do better on whatever it needed help on.

Where do you see yourself in ten years?
I would like to continue blogging, cooking, and traveling in ten years.

Who has helped you most on your journey and how?
I have had help from my whole family on my cooking experiences because they all know how to cook food. But mostly I have had an equal amount of help from my mom and dad when learning to cook.

What is your favorite cooking tool and why?
I think my favorite cooking tool would be this garlic roller that I have. My grandparents gave it to me, and it is really cool. It is a small rubber tube, and you put the garlic clove in it. Then you roll your hand over it, back and forth, and it takes the skin off the garlic for you. It's not something you would have thought you needed, but it comes in handy!

Describe your perfect meal.
If I had to choose a single favorite meal, it would be a rib eye steak, cooked medium rare, with a balsamic vinegar reduction on top and a little truffle oil as well. If you have never tried this, you need to! I didn't think I would like it, but when you put all those flavors together, they are great. For sides with this, I would probably choose some type of potato, maybe mashed, and a vegetable. I really love potatoes like hash browns or potato soup, and I have recently discovered that I like sautéed mushrooms.

There is also this veal dish with prosciutto and angel hair pasta on the side that is a favorite. It is so hard to pick just one. Of course, being from Louisiana, I think crabs and crawfish are up there pretty high on the list as well!

Michael Prados's Recipe
Potato Soup

YIELDS 4 SERVINGS

2 cans chicken broth

1 bag frozen diced potatoes

1/2 cup chopped onion

1 cup water

1 cup milk

3 tablespoons flour

8 ounces shredded cheddar cheese

1/4 cup cooked bacon

1. Put chicken broth, potatoes, onion, and water in a pot.
2. Cover and cook for 10–15 minutes.
3. Pour milk in a small bowl and whisk in flour.
4. Pour milk-and-flour mixture into the potato mixture.
5. Turn up the heat and cook for 6–8 minutes, until thick.
6. Add the cheese and stir until mixed.
7. Take off the heat.
8. Spoon into bowls and top with bacon.

Personal and Private Chefs

Who Hires Personal or Private Chefs?

- Individuals with busy schedules
- Families who don't want to cook for themselves
- Families in which each person wants or needs a different meal
- People with dietary issues that make cooking difficult
- Wealthy individuals who want gourmet meals at home

Whether you choose to pursue a career as a personal or a private chef, here are a few things to keep in mind:

Communication is key. When you sit down with your client and negotiate a contract, discuss specific responsibilities and expectations, including duties beyond cooking. Be specific. Get it all in writing.

Establish boundaries. From day one, keep your personal life separate from your work life. Getting too close to a client makes it harder to renegotiate your contract, decline requests that were not agreed upon, or leave the position.

Be professional. Even if a client isn't your favorite person, maintaining your professionalism will make it easier to work with that client.

Know how to cook for large groups.

Know how to hire additional staff if needed.

Know how to cook for special dietary needs, like vegan or dairy free.

Know how to cook for medical conditions, like high cholesterol or diabetes.

Understand the nutritional needs of your clients.

Pros and Cons of Being a Personal Chef

A personal chef works for many clients. Your main responsibilities are creating menus, shopping for groceries, preparing meals, and properly storing those meals so they can be easily eaten at a later date.

Pros

- You can pick and choose your clients.
- You can choose clients who like to eat what you like to prepare.
- You don't have set hours.
- You can work at your own pace, so it's less stressful.
- You can choose to supply regularly scheduled meals or work only specific events.
- You can be creative, using new recipes and ingredients.
- You can work in your own space and transport completed meals.
- You can cook in the client's home when that person is away.

Cons

- It may be difficult to find clients.
- You may need to work an additional job.
- You will need to advertise and market yourself, which is time-consuming.
- You may have to work for picky eaters, preparing multiple versions of a dish.
- You may have to work with fussy clients who control ingredients, recipes, and ways of cooking their food.
- The lack of a set schedule can be stressful.
- You may have to carry heavy equipment from place to place.
- You may have to work in less-than-ideal kitchens.

Pros and Cons of Being a Private Chef

A private chef works for one family. Often, you live with the family and work out of that home kitchen. The job may include other responsibilities, like managing a budget, grocery shopping, walking the dog, or simple household tasks. Trust is the most important factor in succeeding as a private chef.

Pros

- You get good pay and benefits: 401K, health care, paid vacation, sick time.
- Your salary may include room and board, living in the home or a nearby apartment.
- You may have use of the family car.
- You might travel with your client around the country or even the world.
- You will probably work in a well-equipped kitchen with modern appliances.
- You can be creative, developing new and interesting menus.
- You may get to plan lavish dinner parties.
- You may cook for and meet famous people.

Cons

- The work can be isolating.
- You have to work with the same people every day.
- It may be hard to keep motivated, creative, and learning new things.
- The work can be repetitive.
- Your clients may be picky eaters.
- The hours can be demanding, even requiring you to make nighttime snacks.
- You may have to make less glamorous meals, like lunch for the kids.
- You may have to work within a specific budget.

The Restaurant Business, Owner or Employer

Owning a Restaurant

Did you love to cook as a kid and make your friends play restaurant games? When you pass an abandoned building, do you evaluate it for its restaurant potential? Do you handle stress well and love to work with people from all walks of life? Do you go into a restaurant, evaluate the food and service, and leave thinking you could do it better? If so, owning or managing a restaurant may be the right career for you.

Good chefs don't always make good restaurant owners, but good restaurant owners have an advantage if they are trained chefs. You don't have to attend culinary school to open a restaurant, but a good head for business, a background in business, or some business education would help. If you decide to open a restaurant, you should understand the organization of a kitchen, employee management, business operations including payroll and taxes, as well as facilities management, labor laws, permit requirements, and customer service.

There's a lot that goes into starting a restaurant. Before you consider embarking on this career path, consider the fact that about 25 percent of new restaurants fail in the first year, 50 percent after three years, and about 70 percent in ten years. The statistics seem daunting but are not much different than any small business. If you have the drive, then take the dive!

OLDEST TAVERN IN AMERICA

Newport, Rhode Island, is home to the oldest tavern in America. The building was built in 1652 as a residence for Francis Brinley and his family. In 1673 it was sold to William Mayes, Sr., who turned it into a tavern. In 1703 his grandson, Jonathan Nichols, named the tavern the White Horse Inn. William Mayes's family retained ownership until 1895, when it was sold to Thomas and Bridget Preece. By the early 1950s, the structure was in desperate need of repair. The Preservation Society of Newport County bought, restored, and then reopened the tavern in 1957. A partnership bought the tavern in 1981 and later handed stewardship of it to Paul Hogan. The tavern is over 350 years old, and in all that time, it has had only six disparate owners.

Types of Restaurants

The type and style of restaurant you open is limited only by your imagination. Find where your heart is and go in that direction.

Fine Dining Restaurants. These are the most expensive restaurants. They require reservations and are open for limited hours. They can be large, like those found in high-end hotels, or they can be small and intimate, like those found in renovated houses or old, quaint buildings across the country. Highly skilled chefs, amazing food, and fine wine—it's all about the atmosphere and the customer's experience.

Casual Dining Restaurants. These are less expensive than fine dining but a place where the customer expects a high level of service. They are usually open for lunch and dinner and are often closed a couple of days a week. Good food, good wine, a comfortable atmosphere—it's all about casual quality.

Family-Style Restaurants. These are lower priced, often franchise restaurants. They cater to families and are usually open long hours. Their focus is on offering a predictable menu, fast service, and a comfortable place to bring the kids. Breakfast, lunch, or dinner, they're the place to go when you're hungry.

Diners. Diners are usually found in established neighborhoods. It's the place where locals go to eat a quick meal, chat with their neighbors, or meet up with old friends. The food is "like mom used to make," and the owner recognizes you. A diner's hours of operation depend on the needs of their local customers.

Bar and Grills. These cater to the evening crowds. They are a place to watch sports, listen to music, or meet up with friends for an after-dinner drink. Some focus on serving drinks and the food is secondary, there to meet the requirements of state liquor laws. Others have extensive menus of commonly requested dishes, like burgers and fries.

Buffet-Style Restaurants. Declining in popularity, these all-you-can-eat establishments cater to families and those who want a variety of food choices in one meal. They offer little customer service, stark décor, and a one-price-for-everything cost.

Cafés. Cafés stand alone or are linked to bakeries. Like diners, they draw in local customers and cater to the needs of the area where they are located. Cafés are usually open for breakfast and lunch. They are where people go for a quick breakfast, a meet-up with a friend, or a lunch with fellow workers.

Fast-Food Restaurants. Fast-food restaurants are always chains or franchises. They can be corporate or independently owned. Their goal is to get food to the customer as fast as possible. Most fast-food restaurants have a drive-through window, and everything is served in disposable dishes.

Food Carts and Trucks. Food carts and trucks travel to where people congregate: sporting events, worksites, farmers' markets, or county fairs. They usually serve one style of food, like barbecue, ethnic foods, or burgers. Food carts seldom park in the same place, so their customers must follow them around the area. Food carts feed people who need something to eat on the run.

Food Trucks: A Bit of History

The idea of mobile food began with the first organized military operation. Around the world and throughout the centuries, carts have hauled the rations needed to feed massive numbers of soldiers. Ancient Romans also sold food from carts—on the streets, in the marketplaces, and at theatrical and sporting events, wherever there were crowds of people, ancient peddlers sold their wares. Some carts were pulled or pushed by their owners. Goats or horses pulled others. The bicycle ushered in the age of pedal-powered carts. With the invention of the automobile, cars and trucks took over.

From cupcakes to lobster bisque, creative food entrepreneurs are buying food carts and taking to the streets. Across America, food trucks are becoming a common sight. Luncha Libra in Phoenix specializes in Arizona-style food; Sidewalk Sweets in Washington, DC, serves cupcakes and pies; and Sushi Fix offers fresh sushi to customers in Minneapolis. Need proof that the food truck is gaining in popularity? In 2011, the Cooking Channel launched a reality show, *Eat Street*, in which food truck owners competed to see who could earn the most money. In 2012, the first gourmet food truck opened in Paris. Yes, Paris! Now that's a revolution.

The latest step in the evolution of the food truck industry is happening in Portland, Oregon. The locals call any group of two or more food trucks a "pod," but developer Roger Goldingay took it one step further. In 2009 he opened the first food cart community, Mississippi Marketplace, in North Portland. It is a lot-size settlement and home to ten unique food carts. Two years later he opened Cartlandia, an even bigger, thirty-five-cart super pod in Southeast Portland. These destination pods, now many in number and including A La Carts and Cartopia, were developed to help revitalize neighborhoods and rebuild a sense of community.

Seasoned Profile

Name: Sarah Clements Olivieri
Job: Co-owner, Treehouse Truck, Orlando, Florida

Describe the process you went through in making the decision to open a food truck.
We both had been working in the restaurant industry for years. Vinnie, my husband and business partner, worked

nearly every position in restaurants, and I mainly worked front of house. Owning a food truck had been something we talked about for years. Treehouse Truck was an operating business that went up for sale. We were in the right place, and the price of the business was right. So we dove in and never looked back.

What steps did you take to get your truck up and running?
We were very fortunate to buy a truck already in operation. If we had not, we would have had to build out the entire truck or try and find a food truck and then build the business. When you are first building a food truck, there are many things you need to think about. You need to maximize your space. You are already in tight quarters, and every inch of space should be used for something. If you place all your equipment on one side and do not even it out throughout the truck, you will end up in a lopsided truck. We have seen this done many times, and their trucks are always getting flat tires.

From state to state, licensing varies. In Orlando, you must have your state license, a peddler's license (this is your mobile food license), a food handler manager card, and all proper tags and insurances. Your truck may have been built great, and you might have the perfect menu. Without the proper license and insurance, however, your truck will just be sitting.

Describe an average day in the life of a food truck owner.
Every day, you are running all over town. For us, unfortunately, we are unable to get deliveries to our commissary. At the end of the night, we look over our truck and get our list together of what we need to buy the next morning. We typically get up at 7:00 AM and start the day by answering emails, which is key to managing bookings. Almost everyone who wants to book your truck or have you for an event will email you.

Next we go to the store to get all our supplies—all food, all dry stock, any cleaning supplies we need, etc. From there, we drive to our truck and load it up. After the truck is loaded, we fill the gas and propane tanks. After the truck is filled, we drive to our event. Typically, events run three to four hours. If our event starts at 6:00 PM, we usually start driving by 4:00 PM. That gives us an hour to get to the location and an hour to set up. When the event ends, usually around 9:00 PM, we take an hour to clean up. Everything in our truck gets degreased. All the dishes must be washed. All food products must be wrapped up and properly stored. You need to know how to place everything in the truck. If it's not properly stored, it will fly off the shelves as you drive. After we shut down and clean, we drive back to our commissary. We empty our gray water (dirty water from the truck), fill the truck with clean water, and spray the floors down to clean them. At this time we look over the truck and see what products we need for the next day's event. After this, we head home; typically, it is around 11:00 PM or midnight.

While working, we constantly check our emails. Missing an email is like missing a payday. You have to take care of your personal finances, as well as your business finances. You need to keep track of all your receipts and credit card charges. You need to keep up with payroll.

You are always on the go and always on the road. You will spend a majority of your day driving around. Owning a food truck is very long hours, very little sleep, and you rarely eat. Strange, I know. Our business is very small and we do not have the means to hire help. So we must do the jobs ourselves.

What education/work path did you take to get where you are today?

Vinnie started working in restaurants when he was thirteen. He worked in kitchens, washing dishes, doing prep, and cooking. He eventually moved to the front of house, where he worked as a busser, a host, and a server. Eventually he moved into management. He has worked his way from the bottom to the top in the restaurant industry. He knows the ins and outs. He has more than twenty years of experience.

I have always worked in the front of house as a server. I started in restaurants at the age of eighteen. Working for a high-volume restaurant at Disney, I learned about great customer service and how to deal with high-volume, high-stress situations. Those skills are very important in our business.

Together we make the perfect team. Restaurants and customer service is what we know. It is all we know. It is all we both have ever done. For us, owning a food truck was the next logical step in our lives.

How did you decide on and choose the menu you serve?

Since Treehouse Truck was an operating business, we continued with the same menu theme. The truck already served burgers, fries, and deep-fried sandwiches. Vinnie is originally from Philadelphia, and in Orlando it is hard to find a good cheesesteak, on good bread, with good cheese. So we added the cheesesteaks and chicken cheesesteaks. We get our meat and bread shipped in from Philadelphia, so it is authentic.

Any product you have on your truck, you want to have multiple uses for it. For example, when we added the Buffalo Chicken Philly, we made our own Treehouse Blue Cheese sauce to put on it. Later we added the Bryan's Bruiser, a blackened burger, and used the same sauce. And then we added Bacon Blue Fries that are also topped with that sauce and some bacon. That's how we used one product for three different items.

Being a mobile business, you are constantly driving to find customers. This means our customers are never the same. What sells in one city won't always sell in the other. So we change our menu depending on what city we are in.

The Rachel's Goat Cheese Burger you can't have enough of in one city. In another city, you can't sell even one. It is all trial and error, getting to know your customers.

Describe some events you have catered.
When we cater events, it is not much different from our typical events. We drive up, open our windows, and serve. Some events will have a smaller menu. We will work with the coordinator weeks in advance, pick a few items from our menu, and on the day of the event, they just come to the window and order.

We recently catered a Halloween party. Our clients were having a private Halloween party for family and friends and wanted to offer food to their guests. Instead of having cold meats or soggy sandwiches, they had us come out and serve foods from our menu. It makes it easy on the hosts because their guests are getting good, fresh, cooked-to-order meals, and they get to sit back, relax, and enjoy their party. That was also fun for us. We decorated the truck with a Halloween theme and even carved the cheese to look like jack-o'-lanterns.

What do you like most about owning a food truck?
We like that every day is different. You are in a different city every day. You get to be outside. You are the face of your company and are always meeting people. Aside from the changing scenery, we really enjoy meeting the other food truck owners. We all work extremely hard, and we all know how much pride we each have in our businesses. One of our favorite things is trying all the amazing food from all the other trucks. When we do events together, we will trade food. You truly get to eat some of the most amazing food!

What do you like least about owning a food truck?
We really dislike all the driving and running around. If we were able to get deliveries and have proper storage, our lives

would be easier. Until that is available, the running around continues. You are so limited on space, you can keep only so many products. So, you almost have to go to your supplier every day to pick up product. This wastes your time, money, and gas, and puts a lot of miles on your vehicles.

What advice would you give a young person who might be interested in owning a food truck?

Get to know the industry first. Go to events. Check out the quality of food other trucks are serving. Work on a food truck. Be creative. Find your niche. Most important have fun. Even if you work twenty hours a day and are exhausted at the end of it, always have fun with it. If you don't have fun, you will wear yourself out.

Describe your perfect meal.

Our perfect meal is sitting down together (yes, sitting down!) and enjoying each other's company. We are always together, but we do not always get to enjoy each other's company, and we rarely get to sit down. We enjoy getting out one of our grandmothers' recipes and trying to make it as good as she would. Anything made with love is the perfect meal.

Sarah Clements Olivieri's Recipe

Roast Pork Sandwich Topped with Sautéed Broccoli Raab

Pork shoulder
Olive oil
Garlic, rosemary, oregano, fennel, cracked red pepper, and
  kosher salt to taste
Kitchen string
Broccoli raab
Crusty bread
Provolone cheese

1. Debone the pork shoulder.
2. Lay the pork shoulder open and rub with olive oil.
3. In the opened pork, add the seasonings to taste.
4. Roll the pork up with the herbs inside and tie off into a loaf.
5. Roast the Pork at 250 degrees for 4–5 hours.
6. Blanch the broccoli raab in boiling water for 10–15 seconds.
7. Remove from the water.
8. Sauté on a medium-high heat with olive oil, cracked red pepper, garlic, salt, and pepper.
9. Slice the roasted pork thinly.
10. Serve the pork on crusty bread with sharp provolone cheese and top with sautéed broccoli raab.

Owning a Restaurant

Once you've decided to open a restaurant, you have to answer three questions:

1. Do I want to buy an existing restaurant?
2. Do I want to start a new restaurant?
3. Do I want to buy into a franchise?

No matter what type of restaurant you choose, here are some of the many things you'll have to do:

- Research, research, research.
- Choose the type of restaurant.
- Choose a name and register it with the state.
- Form a business plan.
- Look into financing.
- Understand and apply for licenses and permits.
- Choose a location.
- Design the interior and exterior of the restaurant.
- Create a menu.

- Buy kitchen equipment and furniture.
- Hire and train a chef, sous chef, and staff.
- Get acquainted with area suppliers and farmers.
- Advertise.

Seasoned Profile

Name: Lili Zamani
Job: Former owner and manager of six restaurants, Portland, Oregon

When did you and your two brothers first decide to focus on opening restaurants?

We actually didn't start with a restaurant. The first business we opened was Electric Beach in southeast Portland. We wanted to do something that no one else had done, so we combined a deli with a tanning salon and a beauty salon. We also sold and supported tanning beds in other area businesses. Then we opened the first for-women-only fitness and health club. Maybe ten years later, we opened our first restaurant, Zeba, in Northwest Portland. We served Mediterranean food, all made from scratch. After Zeba, we opened three more restaurants in Portland and two in Missouri.

What role did each of you assume in the process?

I was in charge of everything financial. My brother Ramin chose the concepts and styles, and my other brother Ali was the promoter. We worked together on the locations, since that is the number one consideration in opening any restaurant. We were all involved in getting the restaurants opened. Our restaurants were all fine dining, and we always had some kind of water theme. We built waterfalls, and in one we had a baby shark in a tank. We focused on making them profitable, and then we sold them. The longest we had any restaurant was about two years. Gorilla was the only restaurant that I handled all on my own.

Fast Food: A Timeline

1848   George G. Foster coins the phrase *fast food*.

1921   White Castle opens in Wichita, Kansas.

1921   Pig Stand is the first drive-in restaurant in Dallas, Texas.

1923   A&W opens in Sacramento, California.

1930s   Drive-up windows come onto the scene.

1932   Krystal opens in Chattanooga, Tennessee.

1940   McDonalds opens in San Bernardino, California.

1940   Dairy Queen opens in Joliet, Illinois.

1941   Carl's Jr. opens in Anaheim, California.

1945   Baskin Robbins opens in Glendale, California.

1948   In-N-Out Burger opens in Baldwin Park, California.

1950s   The drive-through speaker system arrives.

1950s   Frozen television dinners appear in the grocery stores.

1950   Dunkin' Donuts opens in Quincy, Massachusetts.

1951   The term *fast food* appears in *Merriam-Webster's Dictionary*.

1952   Kentucky Fried Chicken (KFC) opens in Salt Lake City, Utah.

1953   Burger King opens in Jacksonville, Florida.

1956   Interstate Commerce Act passes; 46,000 miles of road are built. This is the start of the fast-food explosion.

1960   Hardee's opens in Greenville, North Carolina.

1962   Taco Bell opens in Los Angeles, California.

1964   Arby's opens in Boardman, Ohio.

1965   Subway opens in Bridgeport, Connecticut.

Since Gorilla was your baby, let's talk about that restaurant. Discuss the process you went through when deciding to open it.

It was supposed to be my son's restaurant. I would finance it, and he was free to open any kind of restaurant he wanted. When we got to the remodeling stage, he changed his mind. He didn't want to do it anymore. By that time, it was too late—I had the lease. So I went ahead and opened it myself.

Tell a bit about the process you went through in opening Gorilla.

First I registered the name with the state. The idea for Gorilla came when I saw a picture of two baby gorillas on a branch. They caught my eye—captured my heart. They were so gorgeous! After choosing that name, it was easy to decide that the Amazon would be the theme for the decor and everything else. I also wanted kids to come and enjoy this restaurant. Gorilla was the only restaurant that was family dining rather than fine dining.

After the name, I applied for a permit to start a restaurant. That requires drawing up the plans for renovations and upgrades, including any changes I wanted to make to the building or the interior. The county has to review and approve everything, including where the kitchen will be, where everything will be stored, everything, down to the last detail. Back then, it cost me $15,000 dollars just to get permission to open a restaurant at that location and permission to do the renovations.

Once the county gave the go-ahead, we did the renovations, exactly as they were written in the plans, no changes along the way. The work was inspected every step of the way. When the major renovations were done, we worked on the details, the decor, the furniture, and everything else. After it was all done, I had to get an occupancy permit.

While the renovations were going on, I interviewed chefs, sous chefs, cooks, and all the other staff. I trained the chefs and cooks using my own recipes. I had them practice over and over until the recipes tasted just like mine. Once they achieved that, then I knew they understood the essence of the flavors I wanted. From there they were free to experiment and cook what they wanted.

Before Gorilla opened, I kept everything a secret. I covered the windows and swore every worker to secrecy. When we were ready, we uncovered the windows at night and in the morning, we opened. This was the only restaurant that never had a grand opening. We didn't need it. It was popular from day one.

You said that the recipes were your own. Explain how you learned to cook and create recipes.
When I was little, six or eight, I didn't play with dolls. I played cook. I liked to watch what my mom cooked. Then when she wasn't around, I'd sneak into the kitchen and take some of the ingredients. I wasn't allowed to play with the stove, so I took a blanket and set up my kitchen under the trees. I had a small camping stove. I cooked on that, mixing the ingredients and seeing what happened. I didn't know what I was doing.

When I was in my teens, my brother asked me to cook for him and a guest. He bought all the ingredients, left them in the kitchen, and told me to make something. It was the first time I was expected to cook a real meal. I found out that all my backyard play cooking hadn't prepared me for the real thing. The food didn't taste good, and my brother kicked me out of the kitchen. From that moment, I felt challenged. No matter what, I would learn to cook.

I'm self-taught. I had a passion for cooking. I experimented, using taste and smell. Over time, I developed my own style and started creating my own recipes.

What did you look for when choosing a chef?

I looked for personality, a willingness to experiment, and someone who was open to suggestions. Lots of chefs are afraid to take chances. They come out of culinary school knowing only one way to cook, and that's what they want to do. A restaurant's menu needs to be constantly changing. Chefs must challenge the customer to try new things, keep them coming back. A creative chef can go anywhere. They will always be in demand.

What do you see as essential elements in keeping a restaurant open?

Number one is money. You have to have at least a year's worth of expenses in the bank, in case of emergency. After that, challenge your customers with new menu items, don't cut on quality and quantity, keep a very high level of cleanliness, and keep everything looking new.

Why do you think restaurants fail?

Two things: employee theft and wasting food.

What advice would you give a young person who might be interested in starting a restaurant?

Start small. Expand slowly. Don't get in over your head. And start only when you are free to give the restaurant 100 percent of you time. It will consume you. Be prepared for that.

Describe your favorite meal.

I love dry-sautéed beef Szechuan from Chen's Dynasty. I've been eating it since 1979, and it still tastes the same. Every time I eat it, I remember the first time I ate it. I love to go there with family or friends.

Why Restaurants Fail

Population density and location. You do not have enough saved money, or capital, to survive for three to six months without a paycheck. Don't believe that once you open your restaurant, the money will come pouring in.

Size matters: the bigger-is-better effect. The highest rate of failure happens in mom-and-pop restaurants. They are easy to start, and that makes them easy to leave when profits decline. Both suppliers and bankers are prejudiced against small restaurants. They see them as a greater risk and are less willing to wait if payments are slow.

Quality of life. Restaurant owners don't balance their lives and burn out. Someone has to watch the business, every day, seven days a week. Eventually something fails: either personal relationships or the restaurant.

Retirement and the failure to plan for it. The ill health of the owner leads to sudden retirement. There is a lack of transition planning. They got into the restaurant, but they don't know how to get out of it. There is no exit strategy.

Owner incompetence. The dream of owning a restaurant has become a reality. But now what? Some owners don't know what to do once the restaurant opens. They lack essential skills to manage it and move forward.

The passage of time. Every restaurant gets old, physically and stylistically. Decor gets old, diners' tastes change, society's habits change, and technology changes. Updating can be tricky, and most restaurant owners don't know how to do it.

Working in a Restaurant

Are you interested in owning a restaurant but know you have to understand the business first? Are you interested in the day-to-day running of a restaurant? Do you multitask well, thrive in high-stress environments, and like working with lots of different people? If so, maybe working as a restaurant manager is good career path for you.

As a restaurant manager, you are responsible for the overall running of a restaurant. You coordinate the kitchen and the dining room, oversee all employee issues including hiring and firing, schedule and train all employees, and in some cases, do payroll. You could also be responsible for tracking inventory, ordering supplies, and managing a budget. Other responsibilities include keeping the restaurant clean, watching for health and safety problems, and complying with state liquor laws. Above all else, you are responsible for keeping the customers happy.

You can work your way into a manager position, but a two-year degree helps, and a bachelor's degree in business management is even better. No matter your career path, it's important that you to get some experience working in the trenches. Get a job in a restaurant; understand how restaurants operate.

A Day in the Life of One Restaurant Manager

9:00 AM   Arrive at the restaurant. Check the work schedules and handle any employee issues. Reply to any emails and phone messages. Check inventory and order needed supplies. Meet with vendors. Pay some bills.

10:00 AM   The staff arrives. Assign duties and oversee set up for lunch. Keep everyone on task.

10:30 AM	Facilitate the preshift meeting. Talk about new menu items and discuss parties or special events. Make sure everyone has what it is needed to get the job done.
11:00 AM	The restaurant opens. Double-check with the chef, bartender, and head waiter to make sure everything is ready.
11:30 AM–8:30 PM	On the floor, visiting every table and dealing with customer questions and complaints. Keep tabs on the kitchen to make sure tickets are moving through smoothly. Watch to see that the wait staff is performing efficiently.
9:00 PM	Assign closing duties. Check out staff as sections close. Cross-check receipts.
10:00 PM	See that the kitchen staff is cleaning up. Oversee dining room cleanup and next day preparation.
11:00 PM	Close the restaurant. Run reports. Check email and get organized for the next day.
Midnight	Go home.

Other Positions at the Front of the House

Sommeliers

Sommeliers are often called wine stewards. No matter the name, if you are a sommelier, you know everything there is to know about wine. Your job will be in a mid-range or high-end restaurant where you will assist customers in choosing a wine to go with their meals. Some sommeliers are branching out into beer too. To become a certified sommelier, you must undergo intense training. Only the best are granted the titles of Certified Sommelier, Advanced Sommelier, and Master Sommelier. To date, around two hundred people hold the title of Master Sommelier.

Bartenders

State, county, and city laws differ on the acceptable age of a bartender. About half of the states require that you be eighteen years old, the other half twenty-one. As a bartender, you are responsible for knowing the recipes for and making all alcoholic beverages. You must make them accurately, quickly, and with little waste. You are responsible for ordering bar supplies and keeping a proper inventory of liquor and mixes. Bartenders also collect payments and operate the cash register. Other responsibilities include washing glassware and utensils, serving food to customers at the bar, and keeping the bar area clean. To be a good bartender, you need to be friendly and enjoy interacting with people. One major responsibility of any bartender is checking for proper identification. There must be no service to any patron under the age of twenty-one. Your restaurant's liquor license depends on this.

Servers

As a server, your primary responsibility is to take a customer's food order, relay that order to the kitchen, and bring the food back once it's prepared. You are also responsible for serving drinks, including alcoholic beverages, and checking for proper identification. Collecting payments, operating the cash register, as well as setting up and cleaning tables are a part of the job. Besides these responsibilities, you are on the front line of customer satisfaction. Being friendly, calm, and patient are important characteristics of the successful server.

Hosts

Hosts greet customers when they enter the restaurant. They handle waiting lists, evenly distribute customers to each server's section, and escort customers to their table. At the table, they usually describe the specials of the day. Other duties include answering phone calls and making reservations. You are the first to greet a customer, and that interaction sets the tone for their entire experience. Being kind and considerate is the number one requirement for this job.

Food Runners

Food runners are there to move food. They assist servers during the busiest hours by getting food from the kitchen to the table before it gets cold or dries out.

Bussers

Bussers clear tables and prepare them for the next customers. They may refill water glasses and remove plates when a customer is finished.

Restaurant Rating Systems

Michelin Red Guide

The Michelin Red Guide's three-star rating system for restaurants is the best known in the world. Michelin publishes guides for most countries and for many major cities, awarding restaurants in each geographic area one to three stars. One star means the restaurant is very good; two means it is worth taking a detour to eat there; and three stars means it is exceptional and a destination all its own. Michelin uses professional inspectors who rate not only the quality of the food but also atmosphere, service, quality of tableware, and the overall experience. The Michelin Red Guide was first published in 1900 in France.

Gault & Millau Guide

The Gault & Millau Guide was first published in France in 1965 by two restaurant critics, Henri Gault and Christian Millau. They award points ranging from one to twenty based solely on the quality of the restaurant's food. A rating of ten or below means the restaurant will not be included in the book. The guide has begun to branch out and now publishes guides for seven other countries.

The World's 50 Best Restaurants List

This list is compiled from the opinions of more than nine hundred international leaders in the restaurant industry. There are twenty-six regions around the world, and each region has a panel of thirty-six members. Each member has seven votes, and when all votes are tallied, the best restaurants win. This list is strictly rating restaurants, not chefs or restaurateurs.

Zagat

The Zagat Survey began in 1979 and provides restaurant recommendations based on the opinions of consumers. Zagat has a worldwide network of surveyors who, using a thirty-point scale, rate restaurants on various qualities like food, decor, service, and cost. Zagat covers over one hundred countries and rates all kinds of restaurants from fine dining to family friendly.

COOK

CHALLENGE
Write a Restaurant Review

Even if you're not a budding food critic, you may want to learn how to write an effective restaurant review because it will help you hone your writing, evaluation, and communication skills. Choose a restaurant that you have never visited. Plan on going to the restaurant two or more times; this assures that your evaluation is fair. Visit the restaurant at two different times: once for lunch and once for dinner or the same meal on different nights of the week. On the first visit, focus on how the restaurant operates and how the staff interact with customers. On your second visit, focus on the food. Take notes and answer the following questions:

1. How are you greeted? Do you feel welcomed or are you just another customer? Even if there is a wait time, is the host pleasant and communicating regularly with you?
2. Does your server come to the table and welcome you in a timely manner? Does the server know the menu? Can that person tell you details about various dishes?
3. Do the front and the back of the house work together? Is customer service a priority, and does it appear that everyone is working efficiently?
4. Does your food arrive in a timely manner? Is it fresh and prepared the way you wanted it?
5. Is the plate pleasantly presented? Are the textures, colors, and tastes compatible?

Tips for Writing Your Review

-   Include basic information about the restaurant: its full name, phone number and address, hours of operation, if reservations are required, etc.
-   Pay attention to what other patrons are wearing. Whether established by the restaurant or by the clientele, dress codes say a lot about the restaurant. Alerting your readers to this will enhance their experience.
-   Describe the atmosphere inside the building. Is it bright and noisy? Is it dimly lit and quiet? Describe the decor. Does it match the mood? Tell your readers why you would go to the restaurant. For a romantic date? For a family dinner? For a quick meal with the kids? For an elegant night out with your partner?
-   Talk about the menu. What kinds of food? Is it extensive or limited? Highlight a few of the more interesting items from the menu and any specialties. Is there a kid's

or senior's menu? Are there items for vegetarians or those who want a low-calorie meal? Describe what makes the menu unique.

- Describe what you ordered, what you expected, and what you actually got. Were you delighted, disappointed, underwhelmed?
- When talking about the food, use words that convey detail. Writing something like "the sauce was creamy and smooth with a hint of spice" says a lot more than "it was good." If the food wasn't good, state what was wrong with it. Too salty? Overcooked? Bland?

Unique Dining Experiences

Blue Hill at Stone Barns, Pocantico Hills, New York. This restaurant is on a working, four-season farm. There are no menus. Meals are made from seasonal ingredients produced on the farm or from nearby farms.

Bors Hede, Carnation, Washington. This restaurant is designed to look like a typical fourteenth-century English village inn. The food is made using genuine recipes from the era.

Chanhassen Dinner Theater, Chanhassen, Minnesota. This is one of the nation's largest dinner theaters. It can serve around six hundred guests.

Ecopolitan, Minneapolis, Minnesota. This restaurant serves 100 percent organic food that is vegan and raw.

Fritz's Railroad Restaurant, Kansas City, Missouri. When you eat at this restaurant, don't look for a server. All the food is delivered to you on mini trains.

- While your waiter may have nothing to do with the food itself, the service staff has a direct impact on your overall experience. Evaluate the service from the moment you arrive until the moment you leave. Talk about the hosts, the servers, and any interactions you have with management.
- Evaluate your entire experience. Many of the above elements can be blended into your narrative, or you can keep them in distinctly separate sections.
- Find your own voice. Infuse your narrative with humor, interesting language, descriptive words, and a good dose of your personality.

Ninja, New York, New York. This unique restaurant is designed to look like a feudal Japanese ninja village. Guests are led through a maze of rooms where ninjas lurk in the dark. Ninja waiters entertain you with magic tricks.

Opaque—Dining in the Dark, Los Angeles, San Francisco, San Diego, New York, and Dallas. In this restaurant, you eat in the dark. It's supposed to be a sensory experience where the entire focus is on the taste, texture, and aroma of the food.

Oregon Public House, Portland, Oregon; and Cause—The PhilanthroPub, Washington, DC. Both restaurants are nonprofits that serve local beers, use local food, pay fair wages, and donate all profits to charities.

Safe House, Milwaukee, Wisconsin. This secret restaurant is dedicated to all things spy related.

The White Horse Tavern, Newport, Rhode Island. The oldest restaurant in the United States dates back to 1673.

Careers in the Media

As you flip through a magazine, do images of food catch your eye? Do you wonder how they get it to look so natural, perfect, and delicious? Are you interested in capturing the beauty of food through the lens of a camera? Do your fingers itch to write articles and share your knowledge about nutrition, allergies, or other health-related topics? Would you like to protect consumers from contaminated food? Are you interested in sharing your love for food with a television audience? If you said yes to any of these questions, then maybe a noncooking career in the culinary arts is the place for you.

Writers and Editors

A career as a writer or editor in print or digital media means you work for a magazine or newspaper, either online or in print. There are literally thousands of newspapers, magazines, e-zines, and websites that focus on the culinary arts. What is the one thing they have in common? They need content—someone to write it and someone to edit it. Choosing a career as a writer or an editor means getting a bachelor's degree in journalism, English, or communications. For some jobs, a culinary degree would also come in handy. Above all, you must have a passion for food and all things food related. Some writers and editors work for the publication, while others work on a freelance basis.

If you work as a freelance writer or editor, you can promote you work online by creating content for you own website, food blog, podcast, or YouTube videos. Newer outlets like Pinterest and Instagram are also ways of getting your name and your work noticed. The influence of digital media is growing fast. If you don't have an online presence, you should ask your parents for permission and, if it's okay with them, embrace the digital age.

The line between print and digital media is blurring as more and more Americans turn to the web for news and information, social interactions, and product purchases. Most magazines, newspapers, and businesses have an online presence. The articles they post online can be a repeat of what's in print or new content. Much of the online information is enhanced using interactive elements. If asked, you should be prepared to supply photos, graphics, additional bulleted information, video interviews, and video presentations.

Jobs for Writers and Editors

Local newspapers: Cover what's new and what's happening on the local or state food scene. Some newspapers have a culinary section on weekends in which writers can publish feature-length articles on food-related topics.

National newspapers: Cover the national food scene. Stories can range from First Lady Michelle Obama's Let's Move! project, to famous chefs opening new restaurants, to salmonella outbreaks. If there's a food angle, there's an article to write.

Food magazines: Each magazine focuses on a different aspect of the culinary industry. Find the ones that interest you, focus on what each magazine is looking for, and work within those specifications.

Lifestyle magazines: There is always room in lifestyle magazines for articles that focus on food-related topics like obesity, nutrition, and artisan bakeries or on trends like raising chickens or starting an organic garden.

Journals: If you are interested in the scientific side of the culinary world, then focus your work on new scientific studies, food allergies, or other food-related health issues.

Columns: Within newspapers or magazines, there are often recurring columns where a writer can express opinions or opposing points of view on food-related topics. To have an ongoing column, you must be an expert in many areas of the food business, write exceptionally well, and have a reputation for being fair-minded.

Consumer magazines: Writers and editors who work for these magazines focus their articles on educating the consumer, reviewing and rating products or equipment, and reporting on new or unique trends in the industry.

Restaurant reviewers and critics: Reviewers or critics can work locally or travel to various cities, states, or countries. They eat at a restaurant and then evaluate it for food quality, food presentation, customer service, and overall impression. They write interesting articles that describe their experiences in ways that educate and entertain the reader. Fine dining restaurants, bakeries, street vendors, or even food trucks may come under the scrutiny of a restaurant reviewer or a food critic. Critics may also work as judges on reality television shows that focus on food-related competitions or challenges.

Recipe writers and editors: Recipe writers and editors work for publications, cookbook publishers, or cooking shows. It is a unique style of writing and can be difficult to perfect. You need to be precise and concise, explain procedures in simple ways, and be able to catch even minor errors in the measurements or procedures. Besides those skills, you must write in an interesting style that grabs the reader's attention. A strong background in the culinary arts is important.

Websites and eZines: Writing for websites and online magazines requires the same skills as writing for print newspapers and magazines. There are hundreds of them on the internet and their numbers are growing.

Publishing: Within publishing, there are authors, editors, and ghostwriters. A ghostwriter is someone who gets paid to write a book, but authorship is attributed to someone else. Within publishing, you may write cookbooks, memoirs about culinary movers and shakers, and biographies of chefs or other important culinary individuals. You may also write about health, food history, food science, or anything else food related. There's even room for fictional characters who live, love, and have adventures in the culinary world.

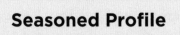

Seasoned Profile

SAVEUR

Savor a World of Authentic Cuisine

Name: Helen Rosner
Job: Digital Editor for *Saveur* magazine, New York, New York

What does a digital editor and food writer do?

I oversee *Saveur*'s digital presence: daily blog content, digital features, social media, and the web versions of print stories. I also make sure our online recipe archive is up-to-date and easy to use, both in terms of design and style, and in terms of commissioning new recipes when it turns out we have holes. (Last winter we were putting together a grilled cheese and tomato soup story, for example, and realized we were missing a tomato soup recipe!) I help with digital special projects: videos, eBooks, iPad and tablet content, and tons of other things that have a digital or web aspect to them, like our Food Blog Awards.

I'm part of a team of four: I work super closely with our digital producer, who takes my crazy ideas and works with our developers and designers to make them reality, and I supervise two assistant editors. We also have an intern team that's usually three college students or recent grads. On a daily basis, I go to a lot of meetings, I do a lot of reading and writing and editing, I take photos and build things in Photoshop, and I make sure everyone on my team is doing good, smart, engaging stuff. I also do a lot of thinking about how people use websites, social media, apps, smartphones, and other digital portals, and what I can do to make *Saveur* better and friendlier and more awesome in all those contexts.

What do you like most about your job?

I love the people I work with. I'm surrounded by incredibly interesting, really funny, really brilliant people who care so much about the world and are so proud of the things they create. It's endlessly inspiring; I learn new things from my coworkers constantly. I also love working on the front lines of editorial technology: it's exhilarating to think about what's going to happen next in the digital world, and I love the thrill of trying to figure out what it's going to be—all the new ways we're going to be able to consume information and culture.

When did you discover a love for food and want to focus your career in the culinary arts?

I'm not going to say I've always loved food, because I'm pretty sure that most people love food, and a good portion of those people love cooking, too. But when I was about eighteen years old, I realized that I didn't just love eating and cooking, I loved *thinking about* eating and cooking: Why am I eating the things I eat? Why does my grandmother eat different things? Why do my friends eat different things? What does the food I eat say about who and where and what I am? I grew up in a family that kept kosher and believed in whole-wheat bread, and when I was in elementary school, my favorite part about going to a friend's house after school was the chance to eat decidedly nonkosher bologna sandwiches on very non-whole-wheat Wonder Bread. It was clear to me that there was something about the things that my family and I had in our kitchen that said something about who we were, just as there was something about what my friend and her family had in their kitchen that said something about them. For me, being interested in food is fundamentally being interested in people—I just happen to think food is one of the most interesting frames through which to view them.

What education/work path did you take to get where you are today?

I had a pretty roundabout path to where I am. I never worked for a school newspaper or took a journalism course—the closest I ever came was taking a lot of poetry workshops in college. I majored in logic and philosophy, which is almost like being a math major, and I was planning to go to law school after taking a year or two to get my bearings after graduation. I very randomly landed a job working for a small, totally non-food-related journalism nonprofit, which wasn't really right for me, and so I sent out probably hundreds of resumes to book and magazine publishers, because

I knew I was a strong writer. I wound up getting a job offer to be the editorial assistant to Suzanne Rafer, the legendary cookbook editor at Workman Publishing. I worked there for three years, pitching in on dozens of cookbooks, learning the ropes, getting into the food world, and honing my line-editing skills, until finally a frustration with the slow pace of book publishing led me to the other end of the spectrum: blogging. I became an editor for *New York Magazine*'s Grub Street blog, covering all sorts of restaurant news. There I worked with another editor, also legendary: Aileen Gallagher, who oversaw all the Grub Street bloggers and basically gave me a full and brutal journalism education in my first six months on the job. She totally whipped me into shape and taught me nearly everything I know about journalism. After three years there, I came to *Saveur*. I never did wind up going to law school.

Food Magazines: A Timeline

1941	Gourmet
1956	Bon Appétit
1967	Nation's Restaurant News
1976	Wine Spectator
1978	Food & Wine
1987	Cooking Light
1988	Food Arts
1991	Martha Stewart Living
1993	Cook's Illustrated
1994	Saveur
1994	Fine Cooking
2001	Gastronomica
2003	Everyday Food
2005	Every Day with Rachael Ray
2008	Food Network Magazine

What advice would you give a young person who is interested in becoming a food writer?

Being a food writer is actually just being a writer—food is a topic, not a writing style. And the only way to get better as a writer is to keep writing, to get over the hurdles of writer's block and the fear of editors and the fear of failure. Put words down on paper (or on-screen or on chalkboards or wherever). Write as much as you can, about food but also about absolutely anything else. Read as much as you can, about everything in the world, fiction and nonfiction and news. Ask questions, both to others and, maybe more important, to yourself. And if you can, find a friend you can trust who will read your writing and give you honest, intelligent feedback on it—behind every good writer is a great editor, and having a good editor making you better is something to be tremendously proud of.

What books helped you along your career path?

The books that made me interested in food writing were Jeffrey Steingarten's great essay collections *The Man Who Ate Everything* and *It Must Have Been Something I Ate*, and Bill Buford's masterfully written and paced book *Heat*, which is about Buford quitting his job to work at Mario Batali's restaurant Babbo and then leaving that to go on a journey to find the chefs and teachers that turned Batali into the chef he is today. Steingarten and Buford both have an exceptional ability to educate the reader while still telling a very personal, very approachable, often very hilarious story, which to me is the hallmark of really great writing. I also love the *New Yorker*'s long-form journalism, especially its profiles and science writing—every single one of those pieces is a master class in the structure and cadence of a great nonfiction story that hews to the truth while still having a point of view.

How do you use social media in your work? Is it effective?

I use social media *constantly*. I run *Saveur*'s Facebook, Twitter, Pinterest, and Instagram accounts, and I also have my own personal accounts. They're all invaluable for staying connected with other writers, editors, and chefs, and staying in touch with readers and finding out what they care about and what they want more of. It kills me when brands and magazines and even writers use their social media platforms just for self-promotion—these channels are about conversation! They're about communication! It's about the back and forth! They're incredibly effective if you use them right; I can't imagine where I'd be without them.

What do you see as future trends in your part of the culinary industry?

I work for a brand that began in 1994 as just a print magazine. Now *Saveur* is a print magazine, a tablet magazine, a website, an eBook series, an online video producer, and a major social media presence. I think the world of food magazines has already changed astronomically, and most of that has been moving in a digital direction. I think it'll keep moving that way, with interactivity and community becoming ever more important.

What is your favorite cooking tool and why?

The day I got a pair of metal tongs is the day my culinary life entered a new level.

Describe your perfect meal.

A super briny, super garlicky Caesar salad—old-school style, with uncut romaine hearts—followed by roast chicken with perfectly crisp skin, salt-roasted radishes, and a hunk of crusty bread with great butter. For dessert, chocolate mousse and a cup of mint tea.

Helen Rosner's Recipe
Tomato Sauce with Butter and Onions

ADAPTED FROM MARCELLA HAZAN'S
ESSENTIALS OF ITALIAN COOKING

YIELDS 4 SERVINGS

I could no longer resist this sauce and, frankly, I don't know why I even tried to: food bloggers obsess over it, and they're not a bad lot to base a recipe selection upon. Another thing that blew my mind about this sauce: I am a grated parmesan junkie. I not only sprinkle it over my bowl of pasta, I like to have additional nearby, to apply a fresh coat to the layers of pasta that follow. So you can imagine my shock to find that I liked this dish even more without the parmesan. The flavor of the sauce is so delicate, fresh, and sweet that it needed nothing at all.

28 ounces (800 grams) whole peeled tomatoes from a can (San Marzano if you can find them)
5 tablespoons (70 grams) unsalted butter
1 medium-size yellow onion, peeled and halved
Salt to taste

1. Put the tomatoes, onion, and butter in a 3-quart heavy saucepan over medium heat.
2. Bring the sauce to a simmer.
3. Lower the heat to keep the sauce at a slow, steady simmer for about 45 minutes, or until droplets of fat float free of the tomatoes.
4. Stir occasionally, crushing the tomatoes against the side of the pot with a wooden spoon. Remove from the heat, discard the onion, add salt to taste (you might find, as I did, that your tomatoes came salted and that you didn't need to add more), and keep dish warm while you prepare your pasta.
5. Serve with spaghetti, with or without grated parmesan cheese.

Food Stylist

To work as a food stylist, you need more than experience handling food. You need a background in art and design, an eye for natural colors and textures, and an understanding of the aromas and tastes of a huge number of foods. A bachelor's degree in the visual arts, along with some culinary training, is a good place to start. Food stylists usually work for food photographers or on television or movie sets.

Food stylists focus on how the food looks to the viewer. They take products and, using every trick at their disposal, make them look beautiful and mouthwatering. On television or movie sets, they are the ones who strategically place food where it's supposed to be and make it look natural.

In advertising, both print and film, the main goal of a food stylist is to entice the consumer to stop, look, want, and then buy. When styling food for advertisements, the food stylists must be aware of the truth in advertising laws. The product being advertised must be exactly what the consumers will receive if they buy it. No improvements, no substitutes—the food must be the same shape, texture, and size. Everything that's placed around the main product can be enhanced.

Being a food stylist is a challenging job. Be prepared to work in different places, like corn fields, fishing boats, or even on a mountain top. No matter where you are, you still have to deal with unpredictable foods. At the least opportune times, they like to break, melt, or even change shape under the hot camera lights. But a professional food stylist is prepared for anything.

Examples of Substitutes Food Stylists Use

When the real thing isn't quite good enough, food stylists substitute other foods or materials to make the food look perfect. Here are a few examples of how they do it.

- Use cream instead of milk to get a rich, creamy look.
- Create more bubbles in certain drinks by adding soap.
- Use dye or paint to enhance a food's color.
- Substitute mashed potatoes for ice cream.
- Use motor oil for a better-looking maple syrup.

Name: Susan Vajaranant
Job: Food Stylist and Recipe Developer, Saugerties,
New York

When did you discover a love for food and want to focus your career in the culinary arts?

I've long had a love of food, my mother would say. Since I was a toddler, I was always a good and enthusiastic eater. I started dabbling in cooking around the age of nine but got really serious about it at about age twelve. By the time I was fifteen, I could get a full meal on the table. I have continued to cook for myself, my family, and my friends through the years. I wanted to go to culinary school when I was younger, but my parents didn't think it was a viable career option. So I postponed my professional training for many years while honing my amateur skills.

What does a food stylist do?

I prepare and style the food for editorial photo shoots, food packaging, and occasionally a television spot. It's very important to start any styling job with finding and shopping for the freshest and most beautiful ingredients. You also need to have good tools that you know how to use, so you can execute your job quickly. You need to be proficient in a variety of culinary areas since you might be asked to roast meat, bake pie, make ice cream, grill fish, or bake bread all for one shoot. Typically I will make an average of eight recipes a day on an editorial shoot. There will be different versions of each recipe using different props or shot from different angles.

Where can we see your work?

I work mostly for editorial magazines, cookbook publishers, and commercial food producers. There are a variety of mediums in which food stylists work, including television restaurant ads, food and cooking shows, and even movies.

What do you like most about your job?

Variety, variety, variety! No two jobs are alike. Even the crew differs from job to job, or client to client. Every job presents new challenges to keep you on your toes, and new rewards as well.

What education/work path did you take to get where you are today?

I have a BA in art conservation from the University of Delaware and a BFA in graphic design from Moore College of Art and Design in Philadelphia, Pennsylvania. Surprisingly, both of my degrees have helped me in my field. I have a good rudimentary understanding of food science from all the chemistry I had to take, and I use many of the lessons I learned about color theory, 2-D design, and photography from my art degree. I also have a culinary diploma from the Institute of Culinary Education in New York City. I did an externship at Gramercy Tavern in New York City. I've worked in the test kitchens at several publications. Some of my best experiences were at *Gourmet* magazine, *Ladies' Home Journal*, and *Martha Stewart Living*.

Who has helped you most on your journey and how?

Oh, so many people have helped me in my field! I couldn't say that any one helped me more than another. I assisted many, many food stylists before I went out on my own. I felt like I learned something different for each one. I learned invaluable lessons on how to deal with the client, how to organize and prioritize shoots, resources for ingredients, when to take shortcuts and when not to, and the list goes on and on. I also learned from all the other members of a typical shoot, including photographers, editors, prop stylists, studio managers, and producers.

What advice would you give a young person who is interested in becoming a food stylist?

Get as much experience and exposure to food as you can. Before going out on your own, you should work as an assistant. It's a very different animal being an assistant and being the stylist. Not only assist stylists but also get some experience working in a restaurant. You will never be sorry for the lessons you learn there. Work for a publication or on a television set if you can, or both. Volunteer for things that interest you. For example, many farmers' markets need volunteers. The James Beard Foundation in New York City is always looking for volunteers. Many industry conferences use volunteers, such as the Chocolate Show in New York City and the New York Produce Show and Conference. Many of these volunteer opportunities are posted through culinary schools.

What is your favorite work or cooking tool and why?

My favorite tool is my hands. Sometimes you just can't get a natural look unless you build things with your hands. That being said, a few of my other favorite tools are a chef's knife, paring knife, iced-tea spoon, and cake tester. I use the cake tester as a meat and fish thermometer in a pinch. I use it to move food on set when I can't remove the plate, and of course, I use it as a cake tester.

Describe your perfect meal.

I've been lucky and had many, many, many great meals in my life! I think the best meal would be an international affair starting in Paris with an amuse-bouche of pâté de foie gras. I would continue on to Spain or Portugal for an assortment of tapas as an appetizer. Then it would be off to Italy for pasta, perhaps something like a pappardelle with a wild boar ragù or squid ink linguine with shrimp, scallops, and crab in a light tomato white wine sauce. Next I would fly to Maine for lobster, fresh corn on the cob, and a summer tomato salad with fresh herbs. Off to Brazil I would go for steak and tender little pão de queijo. Of course I would have to go to Thailand for mangos and sticky rice and the best exotic fruits in the world for dessert. Finally I would finish with some lovely chocolates in Belgium!

What do you see as future trends in your part of the culinary industry?
I think there is going to be a continued influence from food bloggers, social media sites like Pinterest, and individuals' photos from smartphones being streamed all over the internet. I think this will affect a trend toward more natural-looking food, or should I say a more editorial look for food, especially on commercial products, such as food chains, and on food packaging. Consumers are becoming very savvy about the visual differences between the products they are consuming and the picture on the box. Along these lines, I think the local food movement and the increase in farmers' markets will have a great influence on the freshness of ingredients available to people. The public will continue to expect to see these ingredients in recipes and on restaurant menus.

Food Photographers

Food photographers often work hand in hand with food stylists. Once the job is awarded, the photographer sits down with the client, asks questions, and tries to understand what the finished photograph should look like. The client usually has a broad concept in mind, the mood to elicit, the feelings to provoke. It is up to the food photographer to take that concept and bring it to life in one finished image.

Using your experience with camera angles, lighting, and background elements, photographers help decide where the shoot should take place. Once on the set, the photographer takes the lead. If the client doesn't supply equipment, the photographer is responsible for renting lighting and hiring a food stylist, models, and any other necessary staff. No matter where the photograph is taken, the main goal is to create a mouth-watering, attention-grabbing image.

Once the shoot is over, the photographer develops the images, chooses the best ones, prints copies of those images, and then presents the best of them to the client. The client makes the final choice on which image will be used. Photographs may be edited either before or after the client makes the choice.

Helen Rosner's Tips for Creating Fabulous Photos of Food

Use natural light. Nothing will make your food look as good as natural light does—not even the most expensive professional lighting equipment. That said, direct sunlight can often be too bright—in many cases it washes out colors and blows out whites. But a north- or south-facing window any time in the middle of the day will deliver even, warm light that shows off your food at its best.

Use colors wisely. The food isn't the only thing in the frame: using plates and linens in complementary hues helps your dish pop. In particular, brown foods benefit from a hit of contextual color; they look especially lovely against blues and purples.

Don't be afraid of a mess. Restaurants might pride themselves on precisely plated dishes decked with tweezer-placed garnishes, but not too many of us actually eat like that at home. Let things be their natural selves: a few crumbs or a smear of dressing can be beautiful if you let them.

Create a sense of place. Use tableware and linens that are evocative of another time or place. *Saveur's* executive food editor, Todd Coleman, has a dozen cabinets full of dishes, bowls, platters, tablecloths, and napkins; he's a master of combining materials and textures to create an immersive visual environment.

Get people involved. Take the food off the table and emphasize its homey, made-with-love feel by having someone present it to the camera.

Think in three dimensions. You might not naturally serve chocolate-chip cookies piled in a vertical column, but stacking them—or any flat food, like pancakes, fritters, or onion rings—is a great way to show off texture and create visual interest.

Get close to ugly foods. Some foods, no matter how good they taste, just aren't attractive. But the closer you get to your subject, the more the visual story becomes about texture and color, rather than pure mouth-watering beauty.

Take something away. Tell a visual story by undoing one element of a perfectly composed picture: take a bite out of a cookie, pick up just one dinner roll from the pan, cut a slice out of a pie, lift one macaroon from the cookie sheet. This technique, which draws its strength from the tension created by a broken pattern, is particularly effective on an overhead shot.

Where Food Stylists and Food Photographers Find Work

Food stylists and food photographers are often self-employed. Working freelance means you can set your own hours and choose your clients. It also means that you need to be good at selling your services. You need to know how to manage a budget, create profitable bids, get along with different clients, and be a professional in all kinds of circumstances. Businesses that employ food stylists and photographers include:

- Advertising agencies
- Cookbook publishers
- Cooking shows
- Food blogs
- Food magazines
- Large newspapers
- Websites

Seasoned Profile

Name: Penny De Los Santos
Job: Food Photographer; Senior Contributing Photographer to *Saveur* magazine; contributing photographer to *National Geographic*

What does a food photographer do?

I organize photo shoots around food subjects and shoot illustrations for cookbooks and print advertising. I'm often sent to parts of the United States or other countries to record food stories, especially old, long-celebrated food traditions. For example, I was recently sent to the Minnesota State Fair to shoot some really old dining halls. They were beautiful and a part of Americana that is disappearing fast. I've traveled to many countries, including Lebanon, Russia, Italy, and Brazil.

When were you first published and where can we see your photos today?

I was first published in my college newspaper, the *Battalion*. It was a daily weather picture. You can see some of my photos on my website, pennydelossantos.com. Otherwise, they're often in *Saveur, National Geographic,* and *Martha Stewart Living.*

When and why did you decide to focus your lens on food?

It started when my editor at *National Geographic* left and went to work at *Saveur.* One day I got a call from him asking if I would like to take an assignment shooting for two stories, one in Chile and one in Peru. I'd be shooting documentary-style pictures like I did for *National Geographic,* only spotlighting the foods in the regions. That was the first time I worked on a story that focused on food and how people relate to it. I loved the fact that I could enter people's lives through their kitchens and local farmers' markets. The energy, the beauty, the stories inspired me. I knew then that this was an area I wanted to focus on in my work.

What do you like most about working as a food photographer?

I love to document common gatherings of people, tell a story through pictures of what inspires them to be in that place at that time. Food is a subject in itself. It tells a powerful story, interesting and complex.

What education/work path did you take to get where you are today?

I got an undergraduate degree from Texas A&M in journalism and marketing. Then I worked as a photographer's assistant in Dallas, Texas, and later in New York City. I left New York City for a time to work for two small newspapers but soon realized that what I really wanted was to be a photographer. I went to graduate school at Ohio University and got a degree in visual communications. At the end of my coursework, I submitted my portfolio to *National Geographic* and got an internship. On my first day there, someone said, "We throw you into the middle of the lake. If you're good, you swim to shore." My first assignment was in the south of France. I worked for them for ten years. I guess I learned to swim! After that, I got a break and landed a job with *Saveur* and that led to the work I do today.

What advice would you give a young person who is interested in becoming a food photographer?
Get a camera and take photographs every day. Find things that interest you, things that you instinctively react to. Then look at your pictures and ask yourself, *What am I reacting to? Why do I like this picture?* Then describe, out loud, what you appreciate about each photograph.

Start a blog, document your progress, and share your pictures. Get other peoples' reactions to them and learn from their comments. Find books, websites, and other blogs by other photographers. See what they are doing. Study what they are doing.

Making a living as a photographer is hard work. Not only is it competitive, but you also have to know how to be manage your time, manage other people, run a business, create a budget, and control everyone's expectations.

What other types of photographs do you take?
I take pictures using my mobile phone. It has a really good camera on it. I believe that the best camera you own is the one you have with you. I practice taking pictures. I explore everything. I exercise my eye. I also love taking documentary-style, story-driven photographs.

Is there something that you would love to photograph but haven't yet?
Yes. I'd like to explore some of the remote parts of the world, like in China or Africa, search for lost cultures that still forage for food, and create meals using what they find. Find community gatherings that we've never seen before and document them.

Whose work inspires you?

Weegee [pseudonym for Arthur Fellig]. He was a New York City street photographer in the 1930s and 1940s. He was known for his unflinching depiction of life on the New York City streets. His black-and-white pictures are amazing.

Irving Penn. His fashion photographs, portraits, and still lifes. They were taken in the 1940s and 1950s but are still beautiful today. Classics. The dinner-table photographs he took for *Vogue* magazine might make him one of the very first food photographers.

What do you see as future trends in your part of the culinary industry?

Food photography is and will continue to explode in popularity. Everyone is taking pictures of their food and posting them on the web. Food is something we can all relate to, something we love.

Describe your perfect meal.

I would be with six of my closest friends. We would be sitting around an old farm table, outside an old farm house, in the country near Rome, Italy. It's dusk, there are candles everywhere, and a chef is preparing our meal. Good friends, good food, and good wine. Perfect!

Penny De Los Santos's Recipe
Savory Oatmeal

YIELDS 2 SERVINGS

Over breakfast with the editor and food stylist for a cookbook I was shooting in Baltimore, I discovered a new twist on my favorite breakfast. Forget the sweet; this oatmeal is all about savory. Inspired by a shoot on artisanal cheeses, food stylist Susan Vajaranant shaved some sharp cheddar on her already-savory oats, and bang . . . holy shizzle . . . heaven. This is the easiest thing on earth to make, and I promise that you'll love it.

1 cup steel cut oats or rolled oats
1/2 tablespoons olive oil
Pinch of flaky sea salt (optional)
Pinch of cracked pepper
Aged sharp cheddar or Parmigiano-Reggiano to taste

1. Bring 2 cups of water to a raging boil.
2. Add steel cut oats.
3. Lower heat to low.
4. Cook slowly for 30 minutes, stirring occasionally. Oats are done when they are soft, unless you prefer them more al dente.
5. Dish the oatmeal into bowls.
6. Add olive oil, maybe a pinch of salt, a few twists of cracked pepper, and a shaving of cheese.
7. Mix it all together and taste.
8. Maybe add a little more oil, a pinch more of salt, pepper, and cheese. . . . Mix. . . . Taste. . . .

■ ■

CHALLENGE
Create a Beautiful Food Photograph

Using the Tips for Creating Fabulous Photos of Food, create a photograph that can be used by one of the following clients.

Your client is an apple farmer. He wants to create an ad for a local farming magazine to advertise a new apple he has for sale. Your job is to take one or more of these apples and create a photograph that makes the reader want to buy them. Use any apples available to you. There are many way to approach this photograph. Try to create a rural, homegrown feeling; visually interpret that dense, crisp snap you hear when you bite into an apple; or focus on the rich, warmth of the fall colors.

Your client is a huge cereal manufacturer. It wants to create an ad to go in a national magazine to advertise a brand-new cereal. Your job is to create a photograph that makes the reader want to buy the cereal. Use any cereal you have in the cupboard. Some things to think about when creating this photograph are: Who is the audience? What feeling does the client want to elicit? What elements should be the focus?

Sprouting Profile

Name: Remmi Smith
Age: 12
Hometown: Tulsa, Oklahoma
Job (when not studying!): Sodexo's Student Ambassador to Health and Wellness; creator and star of *Cook Time with Remmi* and *The Culinary Kid* video series

When did you discover a love for food and want to focus your energy in that area?

I have always loved food. When I was four, I started helping my mom in the kitchen, doing easy stuff like washing vegetables and making salads. When I was about eight years old, I was making full meals for my family. At this point, I was also trying new recipes and doing a lot of research on foods. I found food even more interesting when I learned where the ingredient or the dish came from.

When I was nine, I started my first video series. I wanted to get kids in the kitchen having fun and finding food interesting. Oklahoma has one of the highest rates for childhood obesity. I thought if I could show kids that cooking is fun, they would get more interested in eating healthier foods.

Within a month of airing my first show on my website, I was picked up by a local cable channel, which aired my show many times a week. Schools and organizations started to offer me opportunities to do cooking demonstrations for kids and adults. The kids and adults seemed to enjoy my presentations, and I started to realize, with my love of food, perhaps I could make a difference. I want to link the skill of cooking to improved nutrition.

As a blogger and the star of two video cooking shows, what does an average day look like for you?

When I am filming, it does cause me to have a pretty full week. We usually film on the weekends, so with school and filming, it is a full seven-day workweek for me. The week is pretty full after school, as I am cooking and rehearsing for the upcoming shoot. I do try to keep up with my social media, and I do a much better job when we are not filming.

How do you juggle both work and school?

Fortunately I love what I am doing, and I love school, too. I am a good student, and for the most part, I am able to keep up with the work. My mom, who is my partner, takes charge of my schedule, and she tries to give me weeklong breaks between shoots.

Can you offer some tips for starting an online cooking show?

The internet gives plenty of opportunities to start your own show. With the ease of setting up a website, YouTube, social media . . . the opportunities and avenues are there. The very best suggestion I have is to find partners who want to work with you. I was able to get my second series filmed by offering a small percentage of my business to my production company. Without that partnership, I may have not gotten my second series off the ground. Plus, the other cool thing about partners is they are interested in helping you be successful.

What do you do in your job as Sodexo's Student Ambassador to Health and Nutrition?

Sodexo has been an unbelievable opportunity for me. I work with the executive chefs in Sodexo's five hundred school districts to provide a kid's perspective on nutrition. I am on posters in all of their four thousand schools, and they serve my recipes to three million students in their cafeterias. I represent Sodexo at many of their big events. I have done demonstrations at the National Restaurant Association and National School Board Association, and was recently in Philadelphia giving a presentation to the Association of Nutrition and Dietetics. Sodexo also has a great program for kids called Future Chefs, and I am the face of this program. I am so fortunate to be part of this because it gives me the chance to reach a huge audience and share my thoughts on nutrition.

You have six brothers and sisters. Do you cook for them? If so, what do you make?

Yes, we have a large family, and the kitchen is the hangout

Cooking Focused Television Stations: A Timeline

1980, Bravo
The Bravo Channel started out as a commercial-free premium cable channel. In the early 2000s, it switched its focus to more reality-based programming, which included cooking shows like *Top Chef*, *Chef Academy*, and *Chef Roldé & Co.*

1987, The Travel Channel
The Travel Channel was launched by Trans World Airlines. Its programming originally focused on travel, but today it incorporates many show that are cooking related like *Amazing Eats*, *Bizarre Foods with Andrew Zimmern*, and *Anthony Bourdain: No Reservations*.

1991, TLC/The Learning Channel
At the beginning, this channel focused on educational content. It later changed and broadened its programming to include food-related shows like *BBQ Pitmasters*, *Cake Boss*, *Little Chocolatiers*, and *Ultimate Cake-Off*.

place for sure. Since I am always creating and testing recipes, my siblings get to taste a lot of my food. I also love to be part of fixing the evening meal. I like just about every food, so when I am fixing more exotic foods, I don't always get a high-five from my siblings. When it comes to the family meals during the week, we make a lot of comfort foods like pasta, shepherd's pie, and dishes like that.

Where do you see yourself in ten years?
First, graduate from a top culinary school. Second, publish a series of kid's cookbooks. Third, host a TV show that is

1993, The Food Network

The Food Network was the first network to focus its programming entirely on food. In the daytime, it aired instructional cooking shows, and in the evening, the focus was on reality and cooking-related entertainment shows. By the end of the 2000s, the network had created more than 225 new shows. Today, they have 132 shows airing each week.

2002–2010, Fine Living Network

The Fine Living Network focused on home-related programming. In 2010, the focus changed to cooking and the name was changed to the Cooking Channel.

2010, The Cooking Channel

The Cooking Channel was created in response to the increasing popularity of all things food related. Their show lineup includes 136 individual shows, including many popular cooking personalities like Emeril Lagasse, Rachel Ray, and Bobby Flay.

all about kids and having fun in the kitchen. Fourth, be a spokesperson or be involved in an organization that is focused on the hunger problem in this world. These are my dreams.

Who has helped you most on your journey and how?
My mother, who is also my partner. She loves being in the kitchen and she encouraged me to be part of it. I think she really saw my potential beyond just loving food. She has worked very hard and she tries to make things as easy as possible for me.

What is your favorite cooking tool and why?

My knife. I use it the most in my cooking.

Describe your perfect meal.

Dining out: foods beautifully presented. My favorite appetizer is oysters on the half shell. I like a salad that is fresh and interesting. I usually select a salad with a combination of ingredients that I haven't had before—like combinations of lettuces with different fruits, for example. I tend to love Italian foods, so a capellini with a light tomato sauce. I like bread too, and I love olive oil and balsamic vinegar with it. For dessert, I always go for the berries. If there are strawberries, that's what I get. It is my favorite food of all.

At home: Fresh salad with my homemade Italian vinaigrette. Main dish would be angel hair pasta with tomato pancetta sauce . . . with bread and olive oil/balsamic vinegar for dipping. Strawberries.

Remmi Smith's Recipe

Strawberry Salsa with Baked Tortilla Chips

YIELDS 10 SERVINGS

1/4 cup red onion, diced small

1 jalapeno pepper, minced

1 yellow bell pepper, diced medium

1 green pepper, diced medium

1/2 cucumber, diced medium

1 pint strawberries, diced large

1/2 cup pineapple, diced medium

1/2 cup fresh cilantro leaves, shredded

1/2 cup orange juice

2 tablespoons lime juice

2 tablespoons extra virgin olive oil

Salt and pepper

5 ounces baked tortilla chips/scoops

1. Prepare all ingredients as directed and mix in a bowl.
2. Serve with 7 or 8 baked tortilla chips/scoops.

Bringing Food Entertainment to the Masses

In the early twentieth century, radio was in its infancy and was mostly used to entertain listeners. That changed during the Great Depression and World War II (1933–1945) when many people bought radios and tuned in to listen to the news, especially President Franklin D. Roosevelt's *Fireside Chats*. Roosevelt used these conversations to keep the nation informed about what the government was doing to combat the Depression and, later, to tell them about the progress of the war. Radio and newspapers vied to become the place where people got their up-to-the-minute news.

Over the next decades, television gained in popularity and radio moved into second place. As more and more programming became available, people turned to television for both their entertainment and their news.

1924, *The Betty Crocker School of the Air* In 1921 the Washburn Crosby Flour Company, known today as General Mills, created a fictional mascot named Betty Crocker. Her radio show ran for twenty-four years.

1926, *Housekeeper's Chat* The United States Bureau of Home Economics created Aunt Sammy, a wife for Uncle Sam. For fifteen minutes a day, the radio broadcast her giving advice to women on how to manage their homes and cook.

1946, *I Love to Eat!* James Beard, known as the dean of American cookery, hosted the first nationally televised cooking show. The

Borden Dairy Company's mascot, Elsie the cow, introduced Beard's segment, "I Love to Eat!", on the *Elsie Presents* show. Unfortunately, few of Beard's target audience of homemakers ever saw the show—only 10 percent of Americans owned a television set.

1948, *To the Queen's Taste* This television show was hosted by Dione Lucas, the first female graduate of the famous Le Cordon Bleu Culinary Institute in Paris. The show ran for two years and broadcast from her restaurant, the Egg Basket, in New York City. Lucas was the first to bring French cooking techniques to the American television viewer.

1963, *The French Chef* Julia Child was the first culinary superstar. Viewers loved her for the way she pummeled meat, dropped pots, and unapologetically made mistakes on the air. Dione Lucas introduced French cooking to the American kitchen, but Child popularized it—and cooking shows—by adapting recipes and simplifying techniques.

1968, *Joyce Chen Cooks* Joyce Chen hosted the first nationally televised cooking show to bring Chinese cuisine to mainstream America.

1969, *The Galloping Gourmet* Graham Kerr sprinkled lighthearted humor and mischievous behavior into each cooking segment. The British chef's cooking show was the first to be taped in front of a live audience.

1975, The Swedish Chef The Swedish Chef joined the other Muppets on ABC's *The Muppet Show*. His sketches usually began in the kitchen, where he prepared meals using a myriad of unusual instruments.

1982, *Everyday Cooking with Jacques Pépin* French-born chef Jacques Pépin focused this show on providing quick, simple, and low-cost dishes. He also showed viewers how to make delicious new dishes out of leftovers.

1989, Chef Louis Chef Louis joined other Disney characters in the hit movie *The Little Mermaid*. He was the chef at Eric's castle who tried to cook Sebastian. Chef Louis has appeared in three films and three television series.

1993, *Cooking with Master Chefs* In each episode, Julie Child cooked with a well-known chef in that person's home kitchen. In 1994 it became the first cooking show to be nominated for a prime-time Emmy Award.

1993, *Chef!* This BBC sitcom was the first television show to make fun of temperamental chefs and the people who work for them.

1993 and 2005, *Iron Chef and Iron Chef America* *Iron Chef* pitted chef against chef in intense competitions featuring a secret ingredient that had to be used in each dish.

1995, *Ready . . . Set . . . Cook!* This was the first American cooking game show. Chefs and audience members competed to see who could prepare the best meal with ten dollars' worth of ingredients and twenty minutes.

1997, *Emeril Live* Emeril Lagasse's hit show was filmed before a live audience and even included a band. Lagasse is considered the first modern celebrity chef.

1999, *Good Eats* Host Alton Brown explored the customs surrounding foods, where ingredients came from, and the science behind cooking, all with a wicked sense of humor.

1999 and 2000, *The Naked Chef* and *Nigella Bites* Both shows appealed to a younger generation. The two personalities hosting them made cooking hip.

2001, *America's Test Kitchen* The first show to include recipe testing. Although it took a serious look at the art of creating recipes, it was the most watched cooking program on PBS at the time.

2001, *30 Minute Meals* Rachael Ray's cooking/talk show focused on entertaining viewers and showing them how to prepare a tasty meal in thirty minutes or less. This show was the first to focus on a single aspect of cooking.

2002, *A Cook's Tour* Anthony Bourdain traveled around the world searching for exotic and dangerous foods to eat. His other cooking show, *No Reservations*, was very popular in America and around the world.

2005, *Hell's Kitchen* The competition is intense as reality-show host and chef Gordon Ramsay screams and yells his way through a group of contestants.

2005, *Food Network Star* This contest reality show is a battle for the ultimate prize, a cable television show and the chance to make it big on television.

2006, *Top Chef* On this show, chefs are given difficult cooking challenges. They compete before a celebrity panel of judges.

2006, *Spatulatta* The kids cooking show takes to the internet. The two young hosts won a James Beard award for their online instructional cooking videos.

2006, Chef Pisghetti The animated children's show *Curious George* introduced this new character. George often visited Chef Pisghetti and helped him create strange new dishes using ingredients from his rooftop garden.

2007, *Diners, Drive-Ins and Dives* One of the winners of *Food Network Star*, Guy Fieri took to the road and explored hidden eating places in nooks and crannies across America.

2007, *Chowder* This animated television series' main character was Chowder. He worked as an apprentice under Chef Mung Daal. Chowder's goal in life was to become a great chef.

2009, *Strawberry Shortcake* Strawberry Shortcake first appeared on television in the 1980s. This modern animated show has the main character, Strawberry Shortcake, working as a chef in a bakery called Berry Bitty Café.

2010, *The Great Food Truck Race* Seven food trucks traveled from city to city to see who could sell the most food.

2011, *Sweet Genius* Reality television turns its focus on pastry chefs. Hosted by Ron Ben-Israel, chefs create pastries and are judged on creativity and taste.

Beyond 2012, *Top Chef Junior* A Bravo-network show that pits teenage chefs against one another.

Beyond 2012, *Charles the Chef* An animated chef travels around the world teaching children about proper nutrition and healthy eating habits. This show is on YouTube and UNC-TV.

10

Food Scientists in Research and Development

Food scientists work in the food processing industry, helping to ensure that farmers maintain or increase their crop yields. You study the physical, nutritional, and chemical properties of food, looking for ways to improve how we store and distribute it. Some food scientists work for the government, inspecting food processing plants for safety, quality, and proper waste disposal. In the laboratory, you study the chemical changes that happen when food is processed or stored. For example, what vitamins or minerals are lost when a food is cooked and then canned? How do food additives change the taste, color, or texture of food? How can we feed a growing population by producing more food on the same amount of land? Working as a food scientist requires a Bachelor of Science degree in food technology or a related scientific field. To conduct research or to teach, you need a master's or doctoral degree.

Where Food Scientists Work

Food processing company laboratories. Scientists here conduct research that may lead to new food sources or better ways to store food. They also search for ways to improve the life of the foods we eat, from the field to the store shelf.

University laboratories. The scientists who work here try to understand and manipulate the genetic material of plants to make them more productive or disease resistant. They also analyze food to determine the amount of vitamins, minerals, fats, sugars, and calories it contains.

Government agencies. These scientists enforce regulations and inspect food processing plants to ensure the safety of the food supply.

OLD WEIGHTS AND MEASURES

Have you ever wanted to use an old recipe, only to discover that the measurements were vague or confusing? Were there instructions in it that you didn't understand? Here are a few old words and phrases that may help if you decide to recreate great-great-great-grandma's favorite family recipe.

Jigger	1.5 fluid ounces
Gill	4 fluid ounces or 1/4 pint
Penny weight *(based on the (weight of a single penny)*	1/20 ounce
A salt spoon	1/4 teaspoon
A saucer	About 1 heaping cup
A pad of butter the size of a(n):	
Hazelnut	1 teaspoon
Walnut	2 tablespoons
Egg	1/4 cup

How We Preserve Our Food

Drying

Evidence suggests that as far back as 12000 BC, people in the Middle East and other hot regions were drying their food. They used the sun and wind to dry fish, wild game, and domestic animal meats. By the fourth century BC, people in Mesopotamia were enjoying dried fruits like raisins, figs, and apples.

During the Middle Ages, people in colder climates began building small "still houses." Using fire to create heat, they dried fruits, vegetables, herbs, and meat in the house and then stored it for winter. They also used this technique to smoke foods for added flavor.

Freezing

Where the climate allowed, freezing was the favored preservation method. In arctic regions, people froze food on the ice. In other northern regions, they froze foods outside or in caves during the winter. When possible, people used cellars or cold streams to slow the spoiling process of their food. Some took huge chunks of ice from streams and stored them in caves or underground sheds. The ice would keep foods fresh through most of the summer.

In 1834, American Jacob Perkins patented the first vapor compression refrigeration system.

In 1842, American John Gorrie designed a system that turned water into ice. He also thought his system could one day cool homes or hospitals.

In the early 1900s, Clarence Birdseye discovered quick freezing. When ice fishing in minus-40-degree temperatures, he saw that the fish he caught were freezing almost immediately. When he later thawed the fish and cooked them, he realized that they tasted the same as fresh.

Fermentation

Fermenting food probably began with the making of beer around 10,000 BC. The fermentation of vegetables, dairy, and grains turns their sugars into alcohol. The fermenting process creates a more nutritious food by creating additional B vitamins, folic acid, gluta-thione (which is an amino acid), and enzymes needed for digestion and detoxification. In dairy, fermenting releases vitamins B and C and minerals like calcium, magnesium, and phosphorus.

Pickling

This method preserves food using vinegar or other acids. The Romans made a fish pickle sauce called garum. Only a few drops of garum added a strong fish taste to foods. In the 1500s, fish brine arrived in Europe. Later, someone in America decided to add some sugar to the brine and invented ketchup. Fish brine was also used to make relishes, mustards, and chutneys. Worcestershire sauce was discovered accidently when a barrel of relish was left for years in the basement of Lea & Perrins chemist shop.

Curing

Ancient societies used salt to preserve food, packing it in different raw salts to create different flavors. In the 1800s, it was discovered that salts mixed with nitrites (saltpeter) gave meat a red color that was far more appetizing than the natural gray. The salt mixture also inhibited the growth of the bacteria that produces several toxins, including botulism.

Jam and Jelly

The story of jams and jellies begins when the ancient Greeks mixed quince with honey and packed it into jars. Eventually the Romans cooked the quince and honey, which made a thicker sweet treat. Over time, the knowledge of how to make jams and jellies arrived in northern regions where people added sugar to the fruits to pre-serve them.

Canning

Frenchman Nicolas Appert (1749–1841) is called the father of can-ning because he discovered that heating foods in sealed jars kept it from spoiling.

In 1810, Englishman Peter Durand expanded on Appert's idea by putting food in tin cans instead of jars.

In 1851, Raymond Chevalier-Appert patented the pressure cooker to can foods at temperatures higher than 212 degrees Fahrenheit.

In 1864, Louis Pasteur discovered why Appert's method worked to preserve food. Heating kills microorganisms and enzymes, and the vacuum seal created keeps more from entering the food. His discovery led to the pasteurization of milk.

Seasoned Profile

Name: Rachel B. Zemser
Job: The Intrepid Culinologist, Burlingame, California

When did you discover a love for food and want to focus your career in the culinary arts?

I knew when I was eighteen that I wanted to be a food scientist and jumped right into the major my freshman year at the University of Massachusetts Amherst. They had one of the top food scientists in the country. While I was getting my BS in food science, I learned about the Research Chef Association, an organization that brings together chefs and food scientists. They encourage scientists to learn more about the culinary arts and chefs to learn more about food science. Eventually I decided to go to culinary school. I knew that I wanted to bring both a culinary and food science angle to my job.

What does a food scientist do?

A food scientist is involved in all the steps that are needed to bring a product from a marketing concept to a finished product. Food scientists will work on bench-top samples, pilot plant small-batch production, sensory evaluation, quality control, risk assessments, specification writing, nutritional analysis, and even packaging. Every step of the development process of any food product needs to be evaluated to confirm that the product will remain safe and flavorful throughout its entire shelf life.

Would you describe a typical day for you?

A typical day might involve creating samples on a bench or working in the pilot plant to make a test run using several hundred pounds of product. Work in the pilot plant is the step that is taken between the bench-top samples and the actual, final production. Other tasks involve cost reductions, taking an existing recipe and making it less expensive by replacing expensive ingredients with less expensive ones. For example, a cookie that has dried cherries in it may be too pricy as the cost of cherries goes up, but the cookie can be cost reduced if some of the cherries are replaced with cranberries. The ingredient statement may change, but the cost savings could allow that cookie to continue to make a profit.

I have worked for a variety of large and small companies. I worked with Unilever in their microbiology group, and I have also worked at Plum Organics, an organic baby food company. I currently am doing a project with Kraft Foods. I like working for a variety of companies; it keeps my job entertaining and exciting.

What education/work path did you take to get where you are today?

I began by earning my BS and then an MS in food science and, after that, a culinary arts degree. Once I started working, I chose jobs that required me to do work that I enjoyed, like product development or culinary presentations. I also have had to do more tedious quality-control work, but I still enjoyed it and appreciated the learning experience.

You got a master's degree in food science and then went to culinary school. Why did you decide to do that? How did that decision change your career or open new doors?

My parents encouraged me to get an MS immediately after I got my BS degree. I didn't really think much about it, but I am glad I did it right away. It's much easier to go directly from a BS to an MS versus working for a few years and then going back to get an MS. I decided to go to culinary school because in the late nineties I started reading about the Research Chef Association, and I liked the idea of combining culinary arts with food science. After I got my culinary degree and then worked for a few years in restaurants and catering, I was able to get a job as a research chef that combined all my skills. I worked for a sauce company and would demonstrate to the chefs how to use sauces in their restaurant chains. I would also, as a food scientist, develop lots of the sauces as well. I had the best of both worlds.

Who has helped you most on your journey and how?

I have had several great mentors, including Dr. Mike Cirigliano, my first boss at Unilever, a microbiologist. I also learned from Dr. Keith Ito, a microbiologist and leader in the food safety industry in California. He taught me everything about acidified foods and pH control.

What advice would you give a young person who is interested in working in food science?

I always tell food scientists to get a master's degree because while not all companies require it, many do, and those extra two years of school will give you an edge in salary. A master's degree also teaches you research skills that you don't learn as an undergrad. In 2012, there were 350 students in the entire United States who graduated with a bachelor's degree in food science. Considering the number of calls I get daily from recruiters begging me to help them find someone to fill their empty food science position, you would think that someone, somewhere would want to help promote the career and help fill the empty positions all over the country. If food science interests you, then go for it! The jobs are out there.

What do you see as future trends in your part of the culinary industry?

I see processed foods becoming more natural, using only dehydration, heat, salt, and sugar as preservatives. I see consumers demanding more information on how their products are made and where their ingredients come from. I don't see junk food going away, but I do see healthier versions of packaged and processed foods showing up in the market.

Rachel Zemser's Recipe
Walnut Romesco

Romesco is a classic Spanish dipping sauce. In Tarragona, Spain, it is served with calcots, a spring green onion caramelized over an open coal fire, but *romesco* pairs well with grilled fish, chicken, pasta, potatoes, and vegetables. This recipe was inspired by Chef Greg Higgins, a James Beard Award–winning chef who owns Higgins in Portland, Oregon. Romesco can be prepared raw or cooked, and it can be served room temperature or warmed; serving it warm brings out the most layers of flavor.

6 medium tomatoes
4 nyora red peppers, seeded
1/2 head garlic
1 1/3 cups walnuts
1 large onion, minced
6 tablespoons extra virgin olive oil
2 medium oranges, juice and zest

4 tablespoons sherry vinegar
1 tablespoon crushed red pepper
Salt to taste

1. Roast the tomatoes, nyora peppers, and garlic in the oven until evenly roasted on all sides.
2. Blend in a food processor until chunky in texture.
3. Set aside to cool.
4. Grind the walnuts in a food processor until finely ground.
5. Sauté the onions in the olive oil for about 5–7 minutes.
6. Add the orange juice and zest, sherry vinegar, crushed red pepper, and ground nuts.
7. Stir until well incorporated and simmer for 3–4 minutes.
8. Remove from the heat and allow to cool.
9. Puree in a food processor to desired finished consistency. Final sauce can range anywhere from chunky with noted particulates to thin without any particulates.
10. Season the final sauce with salt to taste.

Creating a Food Product

Do you have an amazing food product that wows everyone who tries it? Do you want to produce your product and bring it to market? Do you see dollar signs every time you think about selling your product? Consider the fact that huge corporations spend a lot of money paying highly educated people to come up with new products ideas. If you don't see your product on grocery shelves, there may be a good reason why it isn't there. Before you invest any money, do the following three things.

1. **Do extensive product research.** Find out if your product is already being made. Check everywhere—do a long and exhaustive search. See if it made in the past. Did it fail? Why did it fail?

2. **Evaluate the technical challenges of production.** Make sure you understand the exact cost of producing your product. Are there elements that make it too expensive? If so, you won't make a profit.
3. **Do extensive customer research.** Are there enough people willing to buy your product? Does it have a broad enough appeal so you don't lose money while trying to make money?

If you completed the above three tasks and still want to learn more, then check out Rachel Zemser's checklist to help you overcome some of the challenges you may face as you bring your product to market.

Be a man or a woman with a plan. Do you have a business plan? Even though you and all your friends think your product is fabulous, you still need to market it to get everyone else to buy it. Have a plan that outlines what you will do once you have a finished, manufactured product. Food has a shelf life, and a marketing plan should be put together before the product is stashed and aging in a warehouse somewhere.

Go with the cash flow. If you want to manufacture your product, you need money to buy ingredients, pay a copacker to manufacture and package your food, do microbiological testing, ship, package, store, etc. You will have to use your own personal wealth, find an investor who is willing to take a risk, or get a bank loan. Either way, you need to have money. Unless you live in a state that has a cottage industry law, you cannot make this food in your non-health-department-approved basement and sell it.

Find a consultant. If you don't have any experience making or manufacturing products, you definitely need to hire a food scientist. There are big consulting firms and independent specialists—the key is finding the one who knows how to make your type of product. Not all food scientists can make all food products. You want someone who can breeze through it, not troubleshoot around too much, which can be costly. Interview several consultants and make sure you connect with the one you choose. Creating food gets personal, and you need to find someone you can trust.

Get a nondisclosure/confidentiality agreement. People talk, and the food industry is a small place. Have your lawyer draw up a simple nondisclosure agreement (NDA), and ask anyone you share your idea with to sign it. The guy you told your story to on the plane, your investors, your consultant . . . even your mom should sign it. Signing the NDA reinforces the idea that that person shouldn't tell anyone about your idea—or worse, steal it. But be aware that you cannot patent a recipe, only a process.

Find a testing lab. Find a local certified laboratory that specializes in food testing and develop a relationship with it. Let the people there know what you are planning to do (after they sign an NDA!) and get a general idea of what types of tests will be needed to measure the quality and safety of your product. Have competitor samples tested for water activity, Brix, and moisture, so you know what the industry standards are for that particular product.

Audit the copacker. If you already know who is going to make your product, don't just take that company's word or even a third party's word that the facility is clean and good manufacturing practice, or GMP, compliant. Pay your own auditor and make sure the copacker follows all state and federal regulations. While the copacker is ultimately responsible for anything that leaves the facility, it's still your good name on the line. It's your dream that will be recalled, literally and figuratively, if someone else screws up!

Do you still want to produce your product? It's a big risk, and thousands of products enter the market and fail every single year. But you could be one of the lucky ones. You may have that one idea that the big corporations missed. So get going! Stop procrastinating. Get it out there and produce it before someone else does!

Culinary Scientists

Culinary scientists are food scientists with additional culinary skills. Large food companies often hire culinary scientists as recipe developers, to help improve existing products or create new ones. They work as recipe testers who prepare new dishes and offer suggestions for improving them. Companies also hire them as research chefs who taste and evaluate new recipes and give their opinions on the product as a whole. This may include offering insight into ways to effectively package or market the products.

CHALLENGE
Create Your Own Recipe

Start with a general idea of what you want to cook: a new dessert, a new chicken dish, a new kind of bread. Clear out a spot in the kitchen and collect the following items:

- A few sheets of paper
- A pencil
- Bowls
- Measuring cups and spoons
- Stir spoons and spatulas

1. Gather up all the ingredients and spices you want to experiment with.

2. Bring out a mixer, food processor, blender, or other equipment you may need.

3. Start experimenting. Jot down, on a sheet of paper, the ingredients you use for each trial dish. Be creative. Take chances! You never know what might taste good together.

4. When the dish tastes exactly how you want it, make it again. This time, record the exact amount of each ingredient, in the order used. Note any special processes you used: blending, whipping, folding, boiling, etc.

5. Give your recipe to someone else to make. If that person's dish tastes different from yours, you need to clarify your recipe instructions. This step reveals things you omitted, mistakes you made, or even new ways to improve the dish.

6. When the recipe is successfully reproduced, it's time to write a formal copy.

7. Give your recipe a name. Figure out the number of servings and serving size. Give credit if your recipe is adapted from someone else's—for example, "Adapted from Aunt Susan's Muddy Paws Torte recipe."

8. List pan sizes, cooking times, and cooking temperatures.

9. Record each ingredient in the order it is used. Include amounts of each ingredient. Create and label a separate list of ingredients for each part of your creation. For example, Torte Ingredients, Filling Ingredients, and Frosting Ingredients.

10. Write down detailed, step-by-step instructions for preparing your dish. Create a separate section for each part of your recipe: Torte Ingredients, Filling Ingredients, and Frosting Ingredients.

11. Suggest ways to serve, garnish, and store the leftovers.

12. Congratulations! You have just created your first new recipe. And you never know, it may become your signature dish.

Molecular Gastronomists

Molecular gastronomists are scientists or cooks who investigate and explain the physical and chemical reactions that transform ingredients during or after they are cooked. These cooks use techniques perfected in the laboratory combined with certain foods to create concoctions that fascinate their diners. Sometimes this type of food creation is called experimental cuisine or avant-garde cuisine.

To work as a molecular gastronomist, you need to be analytical, logical, as well as creative. The recipes you create will use tiny amounts of ingredients and must have precise instructions to avoid a culinary disaster.

Elizabeth Cawdry Thomas, an Englishwoman and cookery teacher, was the first to publically use the term *molecular gastronomy* in the title of a 1992 workshop that she and Nicholas Kurti, an Oxford physicist, organized, with the help of Harold McGee, a kitchen-science writer and author, and Hervé This, a French physical chemist, author, and editor for the magazine *Pour la Science.* The workshop, held in Erice, Italy, taught chefs about the physics and chemistry of cooking. The first workshop covered basic food chemistry in traditional food preparations. The chef attendees were skeptical—they saw little use for the information in their kitchens. Over time, the meetings included more innovative techniques and well-known chefs like Heston Blumenthal began to attend. The public face of molecular gastronomy was born.

As a result of molecular experimentation, new and innovative dishes have burst onto the culinary scene. Chef Ferran Adrià uses alginic acid and a calcium bath to jellify liquids into balls. These spheres have a thin membrane that bursts under gentle pressure. When they burst in the mouth, the result is an explosion of flavor. Chef Heston Blumenthal learned that fat holds on to flavors. When one of his dishes was eaten, the flavors of basil, olive, and onion were released, and thus tasted, in rapid succession. If you love to experiment, want to create artistic dishes that amaze, and see the plate as a canvas filled with possibilities, then molecular gastronomy is the career for you.

Name: Maya Schulefand
Age: 18
Hometown: Las Vegas, Nevada
Job (when not studying!): Creator of KidChefOnline.com and *Maya Eats*, YouTube culinary videos

When did you discover a love for food and want to focus your energy in that area?

I have always had a great passion for food. There was really no other choice since I was raised by a mother whose interest in food dictated the types of food that I was exposed to. Food was always a big deal, and she would take me shopping in different ethnic markets in order to purchase just the right ingredients necessary for a recipe. She never packed me a Wonder Bread sandwich for lunch. No, it had to be fresh artisan bread that we would pick up at an early-morning farmers' market before school, or pita bread from one of her Israeli markets in Fairfax, Los Angeles. She would travel at least forty minutes each way from our home in Venice, California, in order to purchase Persian cucumbers for her chopped salad. I was taught that long English cucumbers lacked flavor and only Persian cucumbers would suffice. Every meal was a feast of good flavors at our household, and there was always somebody joining us for dinner. She would feed the entire neighborhood with her potato latkes during Hanukkah, and when there was a party at our home, the entire evening revolved around the dishes that she would prepare. I had the good fortune to travel abroad many times, and this too exposed me to many different foods and eating customs.

You developed a website, kidchefonline.com. What prompted you to start it?

Kid Chef was a natural progression for me—how could it be otherwise when I had grown up with so many food influences? I already knew quite a bit about food and recipes. I remember feeling bothered at times by silly comments made to me by other students, who would snigger at my different-looking lunches. I think that this too prompted me to try and expose other youths to foods that they were not used to eating. I found that my friends had a very limited palate, and their remarks about food became tedious.

Your website has evolved to include a presence on YouTube, *Maya Eats*. Describe that experience and how it came about.

When I did Kid Chef, I was a kid; the idea came about when I was around twelve or thirteen years old. But when I turned sixteen, I thought that perhaps the title and format of the show needed a little updating. That is how I came up with *Maya Eats*. The new show was not about teaching how to cook but about sharing my enthusiasm and interest in food and asking my viewers to join me as I taste different types of foods.

What education/work path did you take to get where you are today?

I attended a magnet school in Las Vegas, where I majored in media communications with an emphasis in broadcast journalism. Even though I had many extracurricular activities, like Kid Chef and musical theater, academics have always been of utmost importance to me. I managed to be valedictorian of my graduating class, and I believe that my dedication and work ethic in everything I do is what got me accepted into UCLA, which was always my dream school.

You are currently attending the University of California, Los Angeles. What are you studying?
I am currently undecided because I can only apply to my major at the end of this school year. I hope to major in communications and minor in film.

Can you offer any advice to kids who are thinking about writing a blog or making videos for YouTube?
Blogs and YouTube videos are such wonderful opportunities for self expression. It's a gratifying feeling to be able to do something you are passionate about and have the ability to simply post it online and get feedback from the rest of the online community. If it is something that interests you, it is likely you will find an audience who will love it too! Don't be preoccupied with the number of views you receive or the number of reblogs. Don't let it discourage you if you don't have very many at first. Just keep posting and make it consistent.

How has social media influenced/affected your culinary journey, and where do you see social media moving and changing in the future?
Social media has been the greatest source for me in expanding my knowledge of the culinary world. I go to YouTube on a regular basis to view recipes, cooking techniques, and tips from chefs all around the world. My culinary journey, of course, would not have been the same without social media. On my website I was able to share my stories and recipes with the vast online community, and I would receive feedback from people across the globe. It always amazed me to think that someone in Australia, for example, found my website and was enjoying it and sharing it with friends. Social networking makes the world a smaller place. I feel that our dependence on social media and networking is only increasing.

Where do you see yourself in ten years?
In ten years, I see myself living in Los Angeles and working in the media field at a news station or production company. I see myself still traveling a lot and experiencing the tastes and flavors of the world.

Who has helped you most on your journey and how?
As I discussed before, my mother has been the most influential person in my life. She is the one who constantly exposed me to delicious and out of the ordinary foods. Still today, my mom's cooking is my favorite restaurant. Coming home to a five-course gourmet meal was not rare. For this reason, it has been quite an adjustment having to eat dining hall food every day. My mom has also influenced me in aspects beyond the culinary world. She is the most motivated and ambitious person I know, and her drive is what inspires me to always do my best.

Describe your perfect meal.
I get this question quite often and still, I cannot narrow down my perfect meal! I am incredibly indecisive when it comes to food because I love absolutely everything. And yes, brussels sprouts and beets are some of my favorite veggies. I have also been a vegetarian for six years now.

11

Industry Resources

Resources for Chefs and Cooks

American Culinary Federation, acfchefs.org

American Personal & Private Chef Association,
   personalchef.com

Chefs Collaborative, chefscollaborative.org

Professional Chefs Association, professionalchef.com

United States Chef Association, uschefassoc.com

United States Personal Chef Association, uspca.com

Women Chefs & Restaurateurs, womenchefs.org

World Association of Chefs Societies, wacs2000.org

World Master Chefs Society, worldmasterchefs.com

Resources for Caterers

Convenience Caterers and Food Manufacturers Association, mobilecaterers.com

International Caterers Association, internationalcaterers.org

National Association for Catering and Events, nace.net

Resources for Culinary Arts Schools

All Culinary Schools, allculinaryschools.com

Chef2Chef, chef2chef.net

Culinary arts programs and career cooking schools guide, cookingcareer.shawguides.com

Culinary arts school search, petersons.com/college-search

Recreational cooking classes and vacation programs guide, cookforfun.shawguides.com

Resources for Culinary Professionals

The American Institute of Wine & Food, aiwf.org

Black Culinarian Alliance, bcaglobal.org

The Food Institute, foodinstitute.com

International Association of Culinary Professionals, iacp.com

The James Beard Foundation, jamesbeard.org

StarChefs, a Magazine for Culinary Insiders, starchefs.com

Resources for Food Scientists

Experimental Cuisine Collective, experimentalcuisine.org

Molecular Gastronomy Network,
   moleculargastronomynetwork.com

Institute of Food Technologists, ift.org

Research Chefs Association, culinology.com

Resources for Kids

Junior Leagues' Kids in the Kitchen, kidsinthekitchen.org

Rachael Ray's Yum-O! yum-o.org

Young Chefs Academy, youngchefsacademy.com

Resources for Pastry Chefs, Bakers, Wedding Cake Designers, and Confectioners

American Association of Candy Technologists, aactcandy.org

American Bakers Association, americanbakers.org

American Institute of Baking International, aibonline.org

American Society of Baking, asbe.org

The Association of Pastry Chefs, associationofpastrychefs.org

Bread Bakers Guild of America, bbga.org

Independent Bakers Association,
   independentbaker.net

International Cake Exploration Societé, ices.org

National Confectioners Association, candyusa.com

Retail Bakers of America, retailbakersofamerica.org

Resources for Restaurant Workers

American Sommelier, americansommelier.org

Council of Hotel and Restaurant Trainers, chart.org

International Council on Hotel, Restaurant, and
Institutional Education, chrie.org

National Restaurant Association, restaurant.org

Society for Foodservice Management Onsite Dining Experts,
sfm-online.org

Society of Wine Educators, societyofwineeducators.org

12

glossary

blanch. To partially cook vegetables by plunging them into boiling water for up to one minute and then cooling them quickly in cold or ice water.

boil. To cook a liquid until it begins to bubble.

braise. To brown meat in fat, oil, or butter and then slowly cook it in a small amount of liquid.

capellini. Long, thin noodles, similar to thin spaghetti.

cartouche. A French term that means "scroll" or "packet." A paper cutout that is placed over simmering food to slow down the loss of moisture.

caterer. The person who supplies food or drink for social or business functions.

Celsius. A temperature scale in which 0 is freezing and 100 degrees is boiling or steaming.

chanterelles. A mushroom with a bright-yellow to bright-orange funnel-shaped cap.

chef de cuisine. An executive chef. The person in charge of a professional kitchen.

chef de partie. A position in the kitchen. This person is in charge of a working station.

chop. A term used for cutting ingredients into small chunks.

commis. Someone who works with a station cook to learn the responsibilities of a station.

commissary kitchen. A licensed and inspected commercial kitchen where food is prepared, but delivered elsewhere for consumption. They are often used to prepare food for mobile trucks, temporary restaurants, and food peddlers who then sell their products to the public.

condiment. Something added in small amounts to improve or adjust the flavor of food, like salt, relish, or mustard.

cookbook. A book filled with recipes and the instructions for how to prepare them.

cookery. A type or style of cooking, like vegetarian or Mexican.

croissant. A moist, flaky pastry in the shape of a crescent.

croquantes. A brittle cake or crispy pastry.

culinarian. A chef, a person who cooks professionally for other people, a professional cook.

culinary. Relating to food and cooking.

deglaze. To swirl a liquid into a pan to dissolve particles of food on the bottom to be used for added flavor.

development kitchen. A fully equipped kitchen where recipes are created and tested. These kitchens are usually located within the campuses of large food production companies.

éclair. A pastry that is shaped like a tube with chocolate on top and cream filling.

externship. It is the same as an internship. A person works for low wages in order to learn a craft.

fast food. Food that is highly processed. The food can be prepared quickly or be ready on demand.

Fahrenheit. A temperature scale in which 32 degrees represents freezing and 212 degrees is the steam point (to convert Fahrenheit to Celsius, subtract 32 from the Fahrenheit reading, multiply by 5 and divide by 9; better yet—have a thermometer that reads both scales).

food scientist. A person who studies the nature of food: what causes spoiling, the impact of food processing, and how to improve foods for the consumer.

garnish. A decorative touch added to dishes and beverages.

haute cuisine. Classic, high-quality French cooking.

ingredients. The individual components in a recipe.

knead. To press and fold dough in order to give it a smoother consistency needed for leavening.

kosher. Foods that are fit and suitable under Jewish law.

locavore. A person who is interested in buying food that is raised or grown locally.

marinade. A liquid sauce that is used to soften and flavor meats before cooking.

marzipan. A sweet paste made from ground almonds. Used between the layers of a cake or molded into ornamental decorations.

meringue. Sweetened egg whites beaten until stiff but light.

mise en place. A French cooking term for having all your ingredients prepped and ready to use before starting to cook.

mousse. A light, rich, sweet dessert made from whipped cream, eggs, or gelatin.

nougat. A chewy candy made using egg whites and honey with chopped nuts or mixed dried fruit.

nutrition. The science of researching foods and their effects on health.

organic. Grown or raised without chemical fertilizers or pesticides or artificial growth enhancers.

pastries. Sweet baked goods.

petit four. A small frosted cake.

poach. To cook very gently (slowly) in a liquid that is hot but not boiling or bubbling.

proof. To check the growth of a yeast dough's rise.

pureé. To mash a food until it has a thick, smooth consistency; usually done by a blender or food processor or pushed through a colander.

reduce. To cook by simmering or boiling until its volume is decreased in order to concentrate flavors.

rest. To let the dough sit for a time before cooking.

rise. To allow dough to sit and let the yeast work.

romesco. A nut-and-red-pepper-based sauce from Catalonia, Spain.

roux. A cooked mixture of flour and oil, fat, or butter that is used to thicken liquids.

sabayon. A light, frothy dessert sauce made by whisking egg yolks, sugar, and wine together over a gentle heat.

sauté. To cook foods quickly in a small amount of fat.

scratch (made from). When used in cooking, means that a dish is made from individual ingredients, not from a package.

serrated. A knife with an edge that is notched like the teeth of a saw.

shaved. Thin layers scraped from foods like hard cheese or chocolate.

sift. To remove lumps and aerate dry ingredients.

signature dish. A recipe that identifies an individual chef. Ideally it should be unique so that an informed food lover can name the chef in a blind taste test.

simmer. To gently cook food in a liquid over low heat so only tiny bubbles can be observed breaking the surface of the liquid.

solilemmes. Sweet yeast bread rolls enriched using eggs and butter.

sommelier. A wine steward in a restaurant or hotel who supervises the ordering, storing, and serving of wine.

soufflé. A baked or chilled light dish made with egg whites.

sous chef. A chef who works under the executive chef and is often in charge of the kitchen.

station. A specific area of the kitchen where specific dishes are prepared.

steam. To cook by direct contact with steam.

sweat. To cook in a very small amount of fat over low heat (sometimes covered) without browning to release flavors and moisture.

test kitchen. A kitchen where new recipes are tested or old recipes are retested when there are changes in the ingredients. Test kitchens are used by television cooking shows and cookbook authors.

toast. To bake in the oven until lightly browned.

toque. The hat a chef wears.

torte. A rich cake, built in layers with cream filling between each layer.

vendor. Someone who sells something.

whisk. To quickly mix air into ingredients; also the name of a cooking tool.

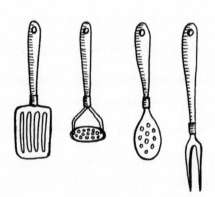

BIBLIOGRAPHY

Websites

All Culinary Schools, allculinaryschools.com

American Culinary Federation, acfchefs.org

Chef2Chef Culinary Portal, chef2chef.net

Culinary Schools, culinaryschools.org

The Food Timeline, foodtimeline.org

Gault & Millau Guide, gaultmillau.fr/historique

HCareers Where Hospitality Works, hcareers.com

The Julia Child Foundation for Gastronomy and the Culinary Arts, juliachildfoundation.org

Michelin Red Guides, michelintravel.com/guides-cat/red-guides

National Restaurant Association, restaurant.org

The Reluctant Gourmet, reluctantgourmet.com

TLC: A Discovery Company, recipes.howstuffworks.com

The White Horse Tavern, whitehorsenewport.com

The World's 50 Best Restaurants, theworlds50best.com

Zagat, zagat.com/about-us

Articles

Ambrose, E. "A Day in the Life: Patrick Higgins, Executive Chef." Last modified February 11, 2012. innsofaurora.com/blog/a-day-in-the-life-patrick-higgins-executive-chef.

Bensen, Amanda. "A Brief History of Chocolate." *Smithsonian Magazine*. March 1, 2008. smithsonianmag.com/arts-culture/brief-history-of-chocolate.html.

Bowen, Dana. "Food of the People: Portland's Food Cart Revolution." *Saveur*. saveur.com/article/Travels/Portland-Food-Trucks.

Bowen, Dana. "The Guide: The Food Cart Pods of Portland, OR." *Saveur*. August 27, 2012. saveur.com/article/Travels/Guide-Portland-Food-Trucks.

Bryant, Charles W. "How to Become a Chef." October 3, 2012. recipes.howstuffworks.com/food-facts/food-careers/how-to-become-a-chef1.htm.

Burton, Jacob. "The Five French Mother Sauces: The Mother of All Resources." Stella Culinary. stellaculinary.com/blog/five-french-mother-sauces-mother-all-resources.

Candice923. "Epinions 101: Writing an Effective Restaurant Review." Epinions. April 10, 2004. epinions.com/content_3862601860?sb=1.

"Candy around the World." The Accidental Scientist: The Science of Cooking. exploratorium.edu/cooking/candy/world-pop1.html.

Carter, Sylvia. "Chef Breaks Code to Ancient Recipes: Babylonian Collections Now the Oldest Known to Man." *New York Times*. May 23, 1985. articles.latimes.com/1985-05-23/food/fo-8362_1_ancient-recipes.

Classic Catering Corp.com. "A Day in the Life of Lispeth Springer, Executive Chef at Classic Catering." October 15, 2012. classiccateringcorp.com/day-life-lispeth-springer-executive-chef-classic-catering.

"Developing a Catering Concept." Food Service Warehouse. foodservicewarehouse.com/education/developing-a-catering -concept/c27512.aspx.

Dudo, Veronica. "A Day in the Life of a 'Top Chef' de Cuisine." May 20, 2011. jobs.aol.com/ articles/2011/05/20/a-day-in-the-life-of-a-chef-de-cuisine.

"Duties of the Prep Cook." Linecooks.com. linecooks.info/ prep-cook.php.

Engelhardt, Chris. "A Day in the Life of Executive Chef Todd Jacobs." *Long Beach Herald.* November 10, 2010. liherald.com/ stories/A-day-in-the-life-Executive-Chef-Todd-Jacobs,28760.

Ferguson, William, and Zahra Sethna. "The Origins of the Cooking Show." *New York Times Magazine.* Based on Watching What We Eat by Kathleen Collins (New York: Continuum, 2009). nytimes. com/interactive/2009/08/02/magazine/20090802_COOKING _INTERACTIVE.html.

Frye, Eva. "A Day in the Life of Absinthe's Pastry Chef, Bill Corbett." *San Francisco Eater.* June 14, 2012. sf.eater.com/archives/ 2012/06/14/a_day_in_the_life_of_absinthes_pastry_chef.php.

GatewayGourmet.com. "A Day in the Life of a Restaurant Manager." Last modified January 24, 2011. gatewaygourmet .com/blog/culinary-career/restaurant-manager.

Goodfleisch, Marcy. "How to Write a Good Recipe." HubPages .com. marcygoodfleisch.hubpages.com/hub/What-make-a -good-recipe-The-best-recipes-will-have-these-elements.

Gray, Amelia. "A Day in the Life of a Pastry Chef." Online Education. online-education.net/articles/hospitality/pastry-chef.html.

Grout, James. "Apicius." *Encyclopedia Romana.* penelope.uchicago .edu/~grout/encyclopaedia_romana/wine/apicius.html.

"How to Write a Recipe like a Professional." The Kitchn. thekitchn .com/how-to-write-a-recipe-58522.

Jacobberger, T. J. "A Day in the Life of Managing a Restaurant." *Inside Scoop San Francisco*. October 8, 2010. insidescoopsf.sfgate.com/blog/2010/10/08/a-day-in-the-life-of-managing-a-restaurant.

Jacobs, Laura. "Our Lady of the Kitchen." *Vanity Fair*. August 2009. pbs.org/wnet/americanmasters/episodes/julia-child/about-julia-child/555.

James Beard Foundation, The. "About James Beard." jamesbeard.org/about/james-beard.

"Let's Make Some Candy!" The Accidental Scientist: The Science of Cooking. exploratorium.edu/cooking/candy/Cando.html.

Lin. "A Day in the Life of a Pastry Chef." BeantownEats.com. September 21, 2012. beantowneats.com/a-day-in-the-life-of-a-pastry-chef.

"Line Cook: A Day in the Life." Line Cook. May 13, 2008. linecook415.blogspot.com/2008/05/day-in-life_13.html.

McGee, Harold. "Modern Cooking & the Erice Workshops on Molecular & Physical Gastronomy." Curious Cook. March 2011. curiouscook.com/site/erice.html.

Mellowes, Marilyn. "About Julia Child." *American Masters*. June 15, 2005. pbs.org/wnet/americanmasters/episodes/julia-child/about-julia-child/555.

Moskin, Julia. "Food Trucks in Paris? U.S. Cuisine Finds Open Minds, and Mouths." *New York Times*. June 3, 2012. nytimes.com/2012/06/04/world/europe/food-trucks-add-american-flavor-to-paris.html.

Nielson, Katie. "How to Write a Compelling Restaurant Review." restaurant-website-reviews.toptenreviews.com/how-to-write-a-compelling-restaurant-review.html.

Nummer, Brian A. "Historical Origins of Food Preservation." May 2002. nchfp.uga.edu/publications/nchfp/factsheets/food_pres_hist.html.

Pillans, Heather. "A Day in the Life of . . . a Caterer." Sun Herald. January 27, 2002. ravioli.com.au/ravioli-articles/2002/1/27/a-day-in-the-life-of-a-caterer.

Project Foodie. "Pastry Chef Carlos Sanchez, Parcel 104." projectfoodie.com/cheflife/cheflife/pastry-chef-carlos -sanchez-parcel-104.html.

Riell, Howard. "Bonus Content—Why Do Restaurants Fail?" *Restaurant Startup & Growth Magazine*. November 2012. rsgmag .com/public/135.cfm.

Rosner, Helen. "Tips for Creating Fabulous Photos of Food." Shutterfly. shutterfly.com/photo-book/storytelling/archives/tips -for-taking-fabulous-food-photography.sfly.

Rossant, Juliette. "The Oldest Cuisine in the World: Jean Bottéro." Super Chef. July 13, 2005. superchefblog.com/2005/07/oldest -cuisine-in-world-jean-bottero.html.

Russo, Lenny, and Barry K. Shuster. "The Economics of Running a Restaurant." Minnesota Public Radio. April 26, 2012. minnesota. publicradio.org/www_publicradio/tools/media_player/popup .php?name=minnesota/news/programs/daily_circuit_3/2012/04/26/ dailycircuitrestauranteconomics_20120426_64.

Samburg, Bridget. "Standing out in the Kitchen: Top Chefs' Headgear Dates back Many Centuries." Boston Globe. July 22, 2009. boston .com/lifestyle/food/articles/2009/07/22/history_of_the_chefs_hat.

Sidney, G. "Failure Rates Recounted: Where Do They Get Those Numbers?" Restaurant Owner. restaurantowner.com/ public/302print.cfm.

So Hearty. "A Day in the Life: Line Cook Edition." sohearty .com/2011/02/13/a-day-in-the-life-line-cook-edition.

Southan, Jenny. "A Day in the Life of . . . Chef de Cuisine." *Business Traveller*. October 3, 2012. businesstraveller.com/archive/2010/ may-2010/special-reports/a-day-in-the-life-of...-chef-de-cuisine.

Spice Blog, The. "Let's Give It Up for the Caterer!" Last modified April 5, 2012. thespiceblog.com/give-it-up-for-the-caterer.

Stahl, Kate. "A Day in the Life: Lockwood Sous Chef Val Benner." PopSugar City. September 22, 2011. chicago.popsugar.com/ Lockwood-Chef-Val-Benner-Day-Life-19162176.

"The Story of Chocolate." thestoryofchocolate.com.

"Toque or Chef's Hat." younggourmet.com/a/32.html.

Weatherford, Jack. "The History of Chocolate." xocoatl.org/history.htm.

"What Is Molecular Gastronomy?" molecularrecipes.com/
molecular-gastronomy.

White, Randy. "The Truth about Restaurant Failure Rates."
White Hutchinson Leisure & Learning Group. Randy White's
Blog. February 24, 2011. whitehutchinson.com/blog/2011/02/
the-truth-about-restaurant-failure-rates.

Books

Hyman, Mary, and Philip Hyman. "Carême, Marie Antoine." In
Encyclopedia of Food and Culture, vol.1, edited by Solomom H. Katz,
320–321. New York: Charles Scribner's Sons, 2002. Accessed in
Gale Virtual Reference Library.

Smilow, Rick, and Anne E. McBride. *Culinary Careers: How to Get
Your Dream Job in Food*. New York: Clarkson Potter Publishers,
2010.

Stern, Jane, and Michael Stern. *The Lexicon of Real American Food*.
Guilford, CT: Lyons Press. 2011.

Thomas, Michele, Annette Tomei, and Tracey Vasil Biscontini.
Culinary Careers for Dummies. Hoboken, NJ: John Wiley
& Sons, 2011.